A-Z BASINGSTOKE

D1766765

CONTENTS

REFERENCE

Motorway	**M3**
A Road	**A30**
B Road	**B3400**
Dual Carriageway	
One-way Street Traffic flow on A roads is also indicated by a heavy line on the driver's left.	
Restricted Access	
Pedestrianized Road	
Track & Footpath	- - - - - - - - -
Residential Walkway	....
Railway	Station / Tunnel / Level Crossing
Built-up Area	
Local Authority Boundary	— · — · —
Posttown Boundary	———————
Postcode Boundary (within Posttown)	— — — —
Map Continuation	**20**

Car Park (selected)	**P**
Church or Chapel	†
Fire Station	■
Hospital	**H**
House Numbers (A & B Roads only)	57 44
Information Centre	**i**
National Grid Reference	4 55
Park & Ride	Leisure Park **P+**
Police Station	▲
Post Office	★
Toilet: without facilities for the Disabled with facilities for the Disabled	▽ ▽
Educational Establishment	
Hospital or Hospice	
Industrial Building	
Leisure or Recreational Facility	
Place of Interest	
Public Building	
Shopping Centre or Market	
Other Selected Buildings	

SCALE

0	¼	½ Mile
0	250	500	750 Metres	1 Kilometre

1:19,000

3 ⅓ inches (8.47 cm) to 1 mile

5.26 cm to 1km

Copyright of Geographers' A-Z Map Company Limited

Fairfield Road, Borough Green, Sevenoaks, Kent TN15 8PP
Telephone: 01732 781000 (Enquiries & Trade Sales)
01732 783422 (Retail Sales)
www.a-zmaps.co.uk

Copyright © Geographers' A-Z Map Co. Ltd.

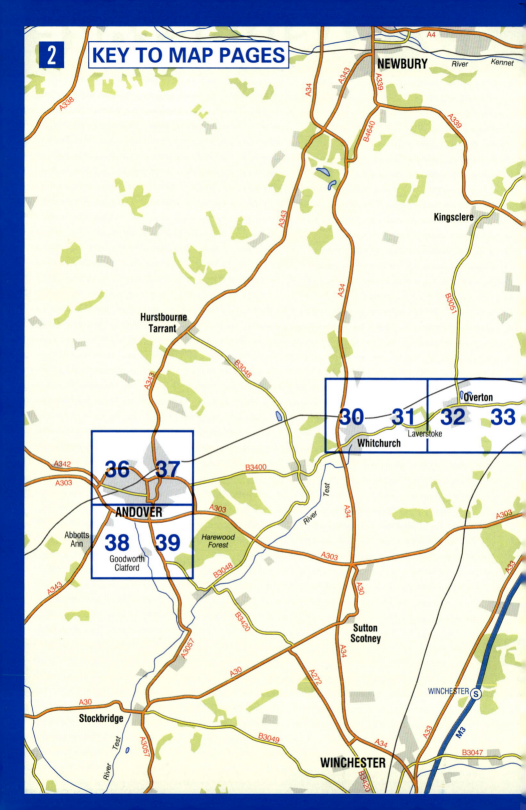

2 KEY TO MAP PAGES

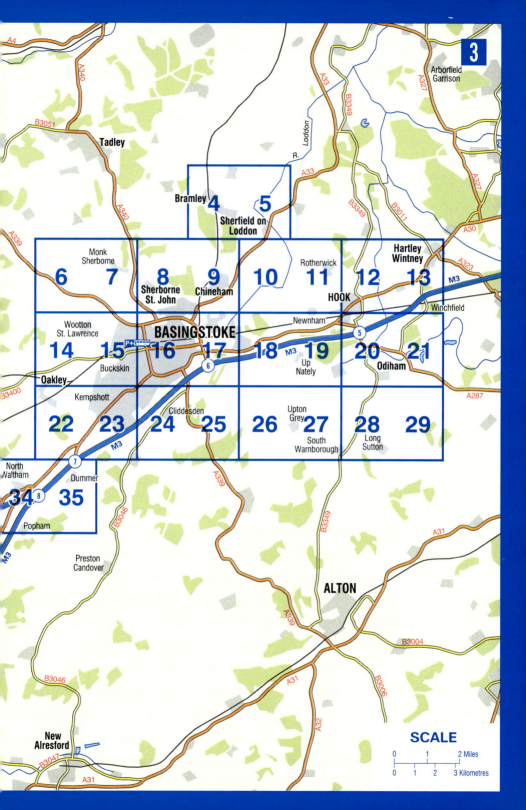

3

A4

A340

B3051

Tadley

A33

B3349

R. Loddon

A33

Arborfield Garrison

A327

A30

A327

A339

A340

Bramley **4**

Sherfield on Loddon

5

B3349

B3011

Monk Sherborne

6   **7**

8 Sherborne St. John   **9** Chineham

10

11 Rotherwick

Hartley Wintney

12   **13**

M3

A323

HOOK

Winchfield

Wootton St. Lawrence

14   **15**   **16**   **17**

Buckskin

18

Newnham

19 Up Nately

M3

5

20   **21**

Odiham

BASINGSTOKE

P+

Oakley

B3400

Kempshott

22   **23**

M3

Cliddesden

24   **25**

26

Upton Grey

27 South Warnborough

Long Sutton

28   **29**

A287

7

North Waltham

Dummer

34 8   **35**

Popham

M3

B3046

A339

B3349

A31

ALTON

Preston Candover

New Alresford

B3047

A31

A32

A339

B3004

B3006

B3046

A31

SCALE

0   1   2 Miles

0   1   2   3 Kilometres

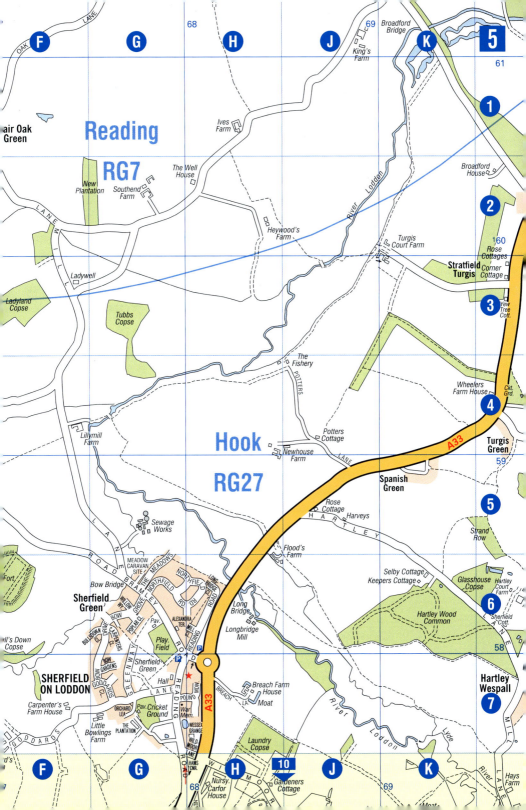

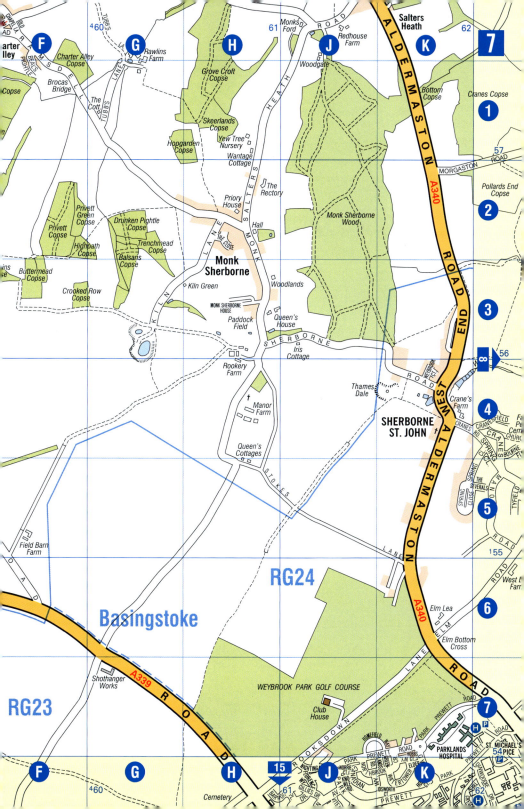

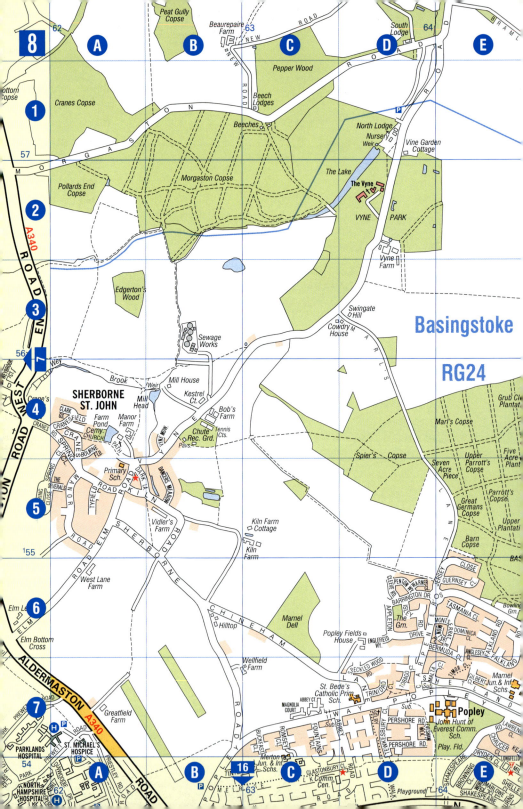

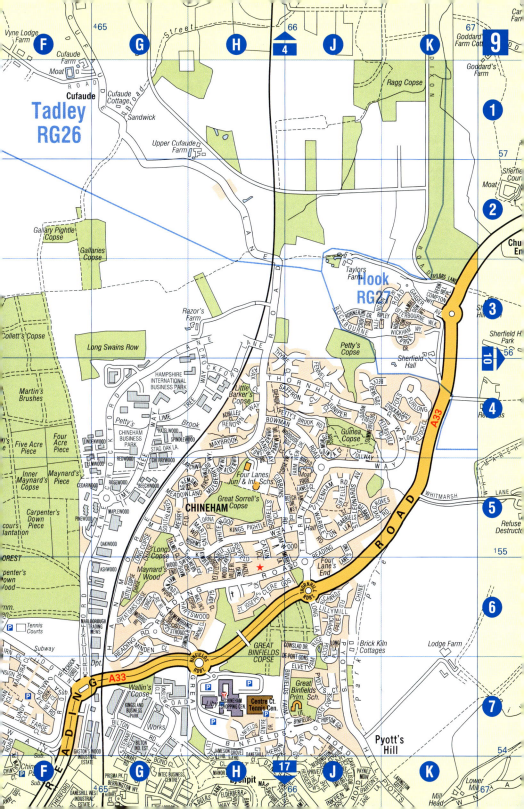

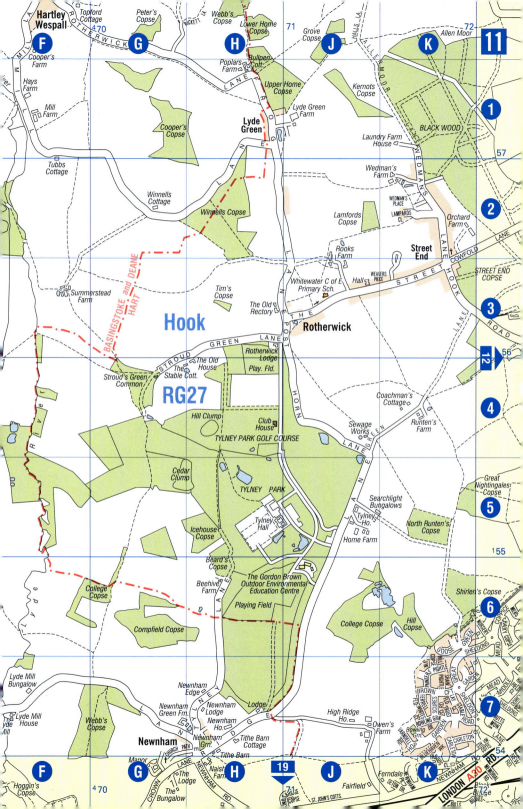

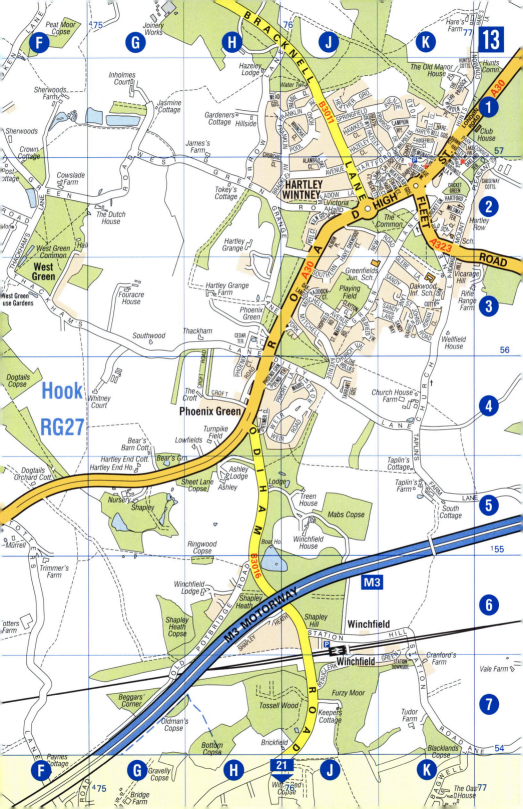

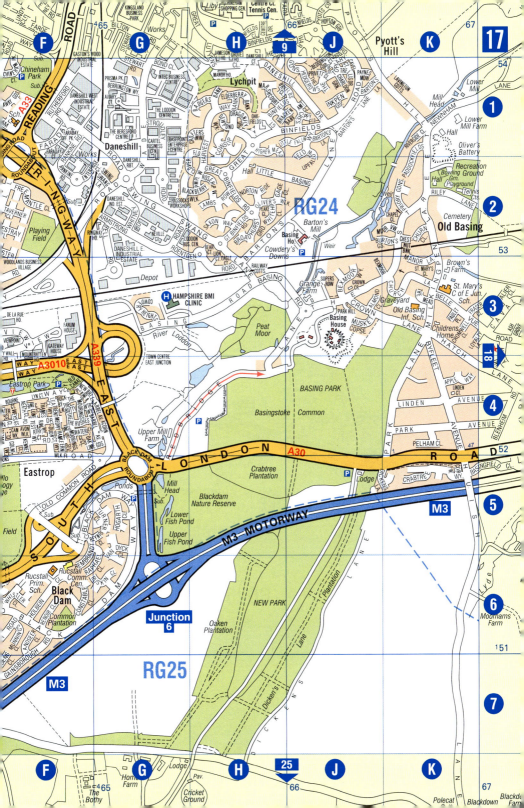

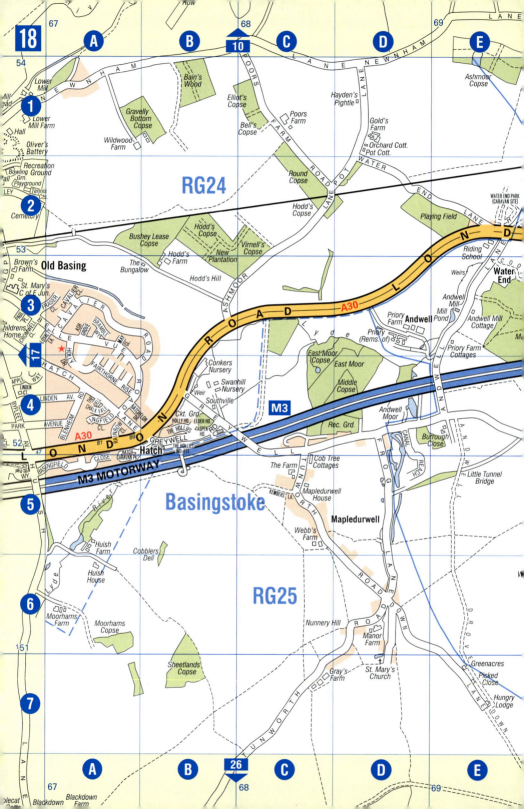

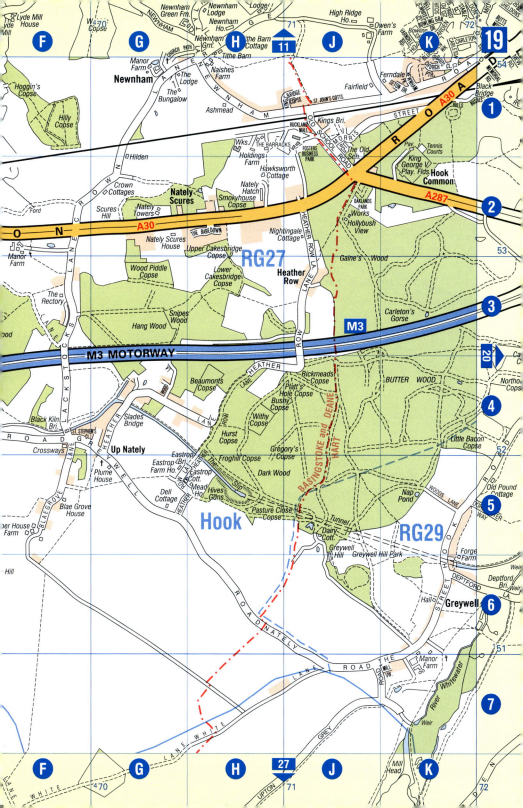

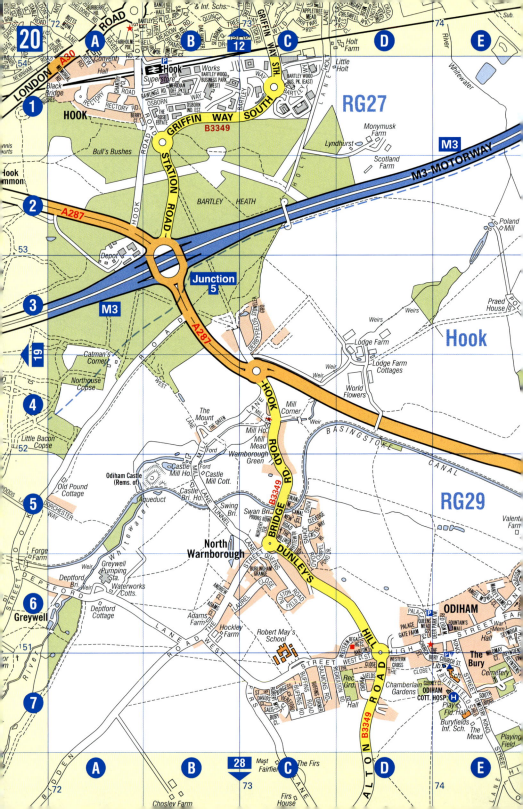

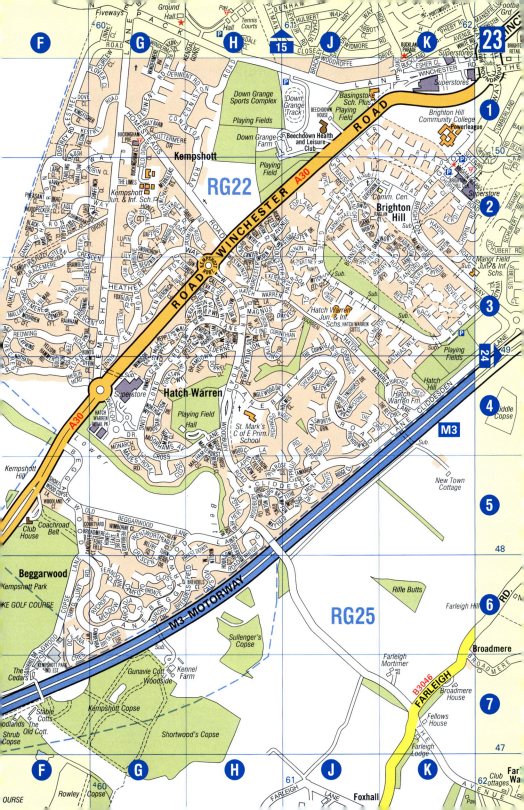

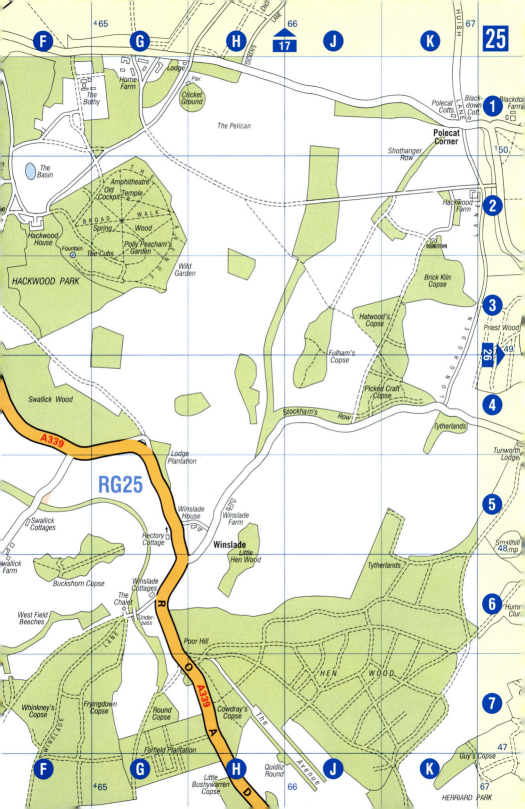

A **B** **C** **D** **E**

67 68 69

18

1

Polecat
Cotts
Blackdown
Cottage

Blackdown
Farm

Polecat
Corner

50

Ragmore
Cottages
Lovely
Cottage

Five La
En

The
Searchlight
Bungalow

2

Hac

DTOWN

Down
Plantation

Sturts
Copse

k Kiln
pse

Tunworth Down
House

Down
Farm

Knights
Wood

3

Priest Wood

Tunworth
Down

Pudding Copse

25

49

Gaston
Copse

Lion's
Row

4

ytherlands

Tunworth

Manor Farm
Cottage
Trelawney

Mayflower
Old Sch.   Cott.
Cottage

Tunworth Hill
Cottages

Upton Grey
Lodge

Lod
Far

Up

Rose
Cottage

Tunworth
Lodge
Manor
Farm

The Barracks

**Basingstoke
RG25**

The Old
Rectory

5

48

Smallhill
Clump

Copse Close
Beeches

Prior's Hill

The Dower
House

6

Hummock
Clump

Tidbury Ring

Tunworth
Belt

Green's Copse

Weston Mark

Weston Mark
Cottages

WESTON

7

Coombe Wood

Hay
Down

The
Board

Reeds Farm
House

Reed
Dell

Middle
Copse

Weston
Patrick Ho.

Haydown

Weston
Corbett
House

47

Guy's Copse

Tom's
Copse

Hook's
Copse

Haydown
Belt

Weston
Corbett

Manor
Farm

Weston
Patrick

Manor
Farm

HERRIARD PARK

67 68 69

The Old
Rectory

A **B** **C** **D** **E**

Hook
RG29

ODIHAM AIRFIELD

ROYAL AIR FORCE STATION

Sports Ground

Snatchange Farm

Chosley Farm

Mast Fairfield
The Firs
Firs House
Clump House
Masts

Down Farm Cottages

Down Farm

Four Lanes End

Middlefield Dell

Six Acre Dell

Hayley Copse

New Cottages

Littlefold

The Old Orchard

S. Warnborough Lodge

Lee's Farm

Lee's Cottage

South Warnborough

Swanshett Coppice

Wells Hill

Wells Hill Farm

Warnborough Park

HESTERS COPSE

Long Sutton

Manor Fm.

The Old Parsonage

The Old Farm

The Old Vicarage

Graveyard

Long Sutton C of E Prim. Sch.

Sutton Warblington

Hydegate House

Lord Wandsworth College

Playing Field

Play. Fld.

Sewage Works

Park Copse

Mem.
The Walled Gardens
Manor House
The Old Rectory
Hall

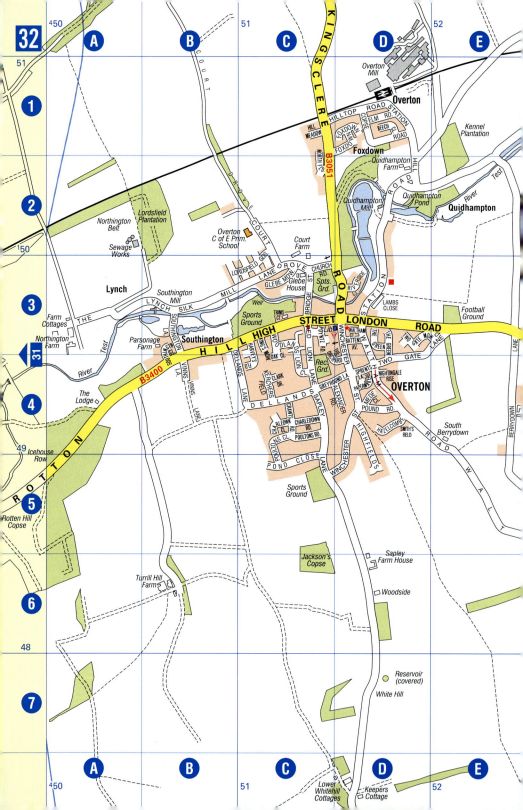

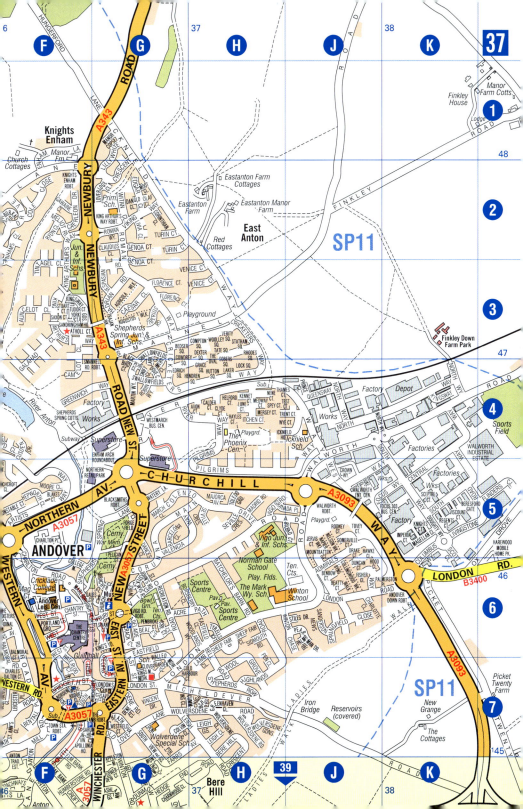

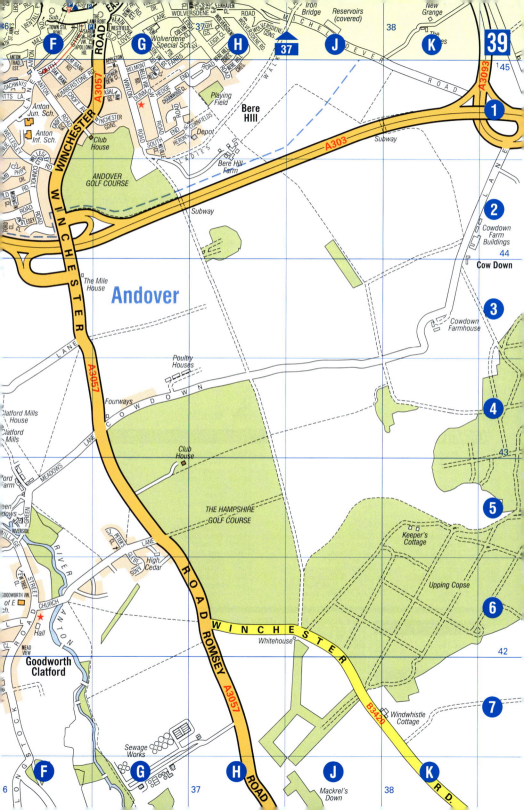

INDEX

Including Streets, Places & Areas, Hospitals & Hospices, Industrial Estates,
Selected Flats & Walkways, Stations and Selected Places of Interest.

HOW TO USE THIS INDEX

1. Each street name is followed by its Postcode District and then its Locality abbreviation(s) and then its map reference;
   e.g. **Abbey Rd.** RG24: B'toke . . . .7C **8** is in the RG24 Postcode District and the Basingstoke Locality and is to be found in square 7C on page **8**.
   The page number is shown in bold type.

2. A strict alphabetical order is followed in which Av., Rd., St., etc. (though abbreviated) are read in full and as part of the street name;
   e.g. **Apple Tree Gro.** appears after **Appletree Cl.** but before **Appletree Mead**

3. Streets and a selection of flats and walkways too small to be shown on the maps, appear in the index with the thoroughfare to which it is connected
   shown in brackets; e.g. **Alders Cl.** RG21: B'toke . . . .4F **17** (off Loddon Dr.)

4. Addresses that are in more than one part are referred to as not continuous.

5. Places and areas are shown in the index in **BLUE TYPE** and the map reference is to the actual map square in which the town centre or area is located
   and not to the place name shown on the map; e.g. **ANDOVER** 7F **37**

6. An example of a selected place of interest is **Andover Mus. & Mus. of the Iron Age** 6G 37

7. An example of a station is **Andover Station (Rail)** . . . .6E **36**. Included are Rail **(Rail)** and Park & Ride **(Park & Ride)**

8. An example of a hospital or hospice is **ANDOVER WAR MEMORIAL COMMUNITY HOSPITAL** 5D 36

GENERAL ABBREVIATIONS

All. : Alley	**Ent.** : Enterprise	**Lit.** : Little	**Shop.** : Shopping
App. : Approach	**Est.** : Estate	**Lwr.** : Lower	**Sth.** : South
Av. : Avenue	**Fld.** : Field	**Mnr.** : Manor	**Sq.** : Square
Bri. : Bridge	**Flds.** : Fields	**Mkt.** : Market	**St.** : Street
Bus. : Business	**Gdns.** : Gardens	**Mdw.** : Meadow	**Ter.** : Terrace
Cvn. : Caravan	**Gth.** : Garth	**Mdws.** : Meadows	**Trad.** : Trading
Cen. : Centre	**Ga.** : Gate	**M.** : Mews	**Up.** : Upper
Cl. : Close	**Gt.** : Great	**Mt.** : Mount	**Va.** : Vale
Comn. : Common	**Grn.** : Green	**Mus.** : Museum	**Vw.** : View
Cnr. : Corner	**Gro.** : Grove	**Nth.** : North	**Vs.** : Villas
Cotts. : Cottages	**Hgts.** : Heights	**Pde.** : Parade	**Wlk.** : Walk
Ct. : Court	**Ho.** : House	**Pk.** : Park	**W.** : West
Cres. : Crescent	**Ind.** : Industrial	**Pl.** : Place	**Yd.** : Yard
Cft. : Croft	**Info.** : Information	**Ri.** : Rise	
Dr. : Drive	**Junc.** : Junction	**Rd.** : Road	
E. : East	**La.** : Lane	**Rdbt.** : Roundabout	

LOCALITY ABBREVIATIONS

Abb A : **Abbotts Ann**	Enh A : **Enham Alamein**	Newf : **Newfound**	S War : **South Warnborough**
A'ver : **Andover**	Far W : **Farleigh Wallop**	Newn : **Newnham**	Stev : **Steventon**
And D : **Andover Down**	Free : **Freefolk**	N Wal : **North Waltham**	Stra S : **Stratfield Saye**
A'ell : **Andwell**	G Cla : **Goodworth Clatford**	N War : **North Warnborough**	Stra T : **Stratfield Turgis**
Ann V : **Anna Valley**	Grey : **Greywell**	Oak : **Oakley**	Tun : **Tunworth**
Ashe : **Ashe**	H Wes : **Hartley Wespall**	Odi : **Odiham**	U Nat : **Up Nately**
B'toke : **Basingstoke**	H Win : **Hartley Wintney**	Old B : **Old Basing**	Up C : **Upper Clatford**
Bau : **Baughurst**	Haze : **Hazeley**	Over : **Overton**	Up W : **Upper Wootton**
B'ley : **Bramley**	Hoo : **Hook**	Pen C : **Penton Corner**	Up G : **Upton Grey**
Charl : **Charlton**	Hur P : **Hurstbourne Priors**	Pen M : **Penton Mewsey**	Wel : **Well**
Cha A : **Charter Alley**	K Enh : **Knights Enham**	Pic P : **Picket Piece**	W Cor : **Weston Corbett**
Chin : **Chineham**	Lave : **Laverstoke**	Rams : **Ramsdell**	Wher : **Wherwell**
Clid : **Cliddesden**	L Sut : **Long Sutton**	Red R : **Red Rice**	Whit : **Whitchurch**
Col H : **Cole Henley**	Lych : **Lychpit**	Roth : **Rotherwick**	Win : **Winchfield**
Dea : **Deane**	Mapl : **Mapledurwell**	Sher J : **Sherborne St John**	W Law : **Wootton St Lawrence**
Dogm : **Dogmersfield**	Matt : **Mattingley**	Sher L : **Sherfield on Loddon**	Wort : **Worting**
Dumm : **Dummer**	M She : **Monk Sherborne**	Sil : **Silchester**	
Elli : **Ellisfield**	Nat S : **Nately Scures**	Sman : **Smannell**	

A

10 Centre, The
　RG21: B'toke 3A **16**

Abbey Ct. RG24: Sher J 7C **8**
　SP10: A'ver 6E **36**
Abbey Rd. RG24: B'toke 7C **8**
Abbott Cl. RG22: B'toke 7J **15**
Abbotts Cl. SP11: Abb A . . .3A **38**
Abbotts Hill SP11: Abb A . . .4A **38**
Above Town SP11: Up C 3D **38**
Achilles Cl. RG24: Chin 4H **9**
Acorn Cl. RG21: B'toke 4G **17**
Acre Ct. SP10: A'ver 6G **37**

Acre Path SP10: A'ver 6G **37**
Acton Ho. RG22: B'toke 5A **16**
Adams Cl. RG29: N War 6B **20**
Addison Gdns. RG29: Odi . . .6E **20**
Adelaide Rd. SP10: A'ver . . .6G **37**
Admirals Way SP10: A'ver . . .6J **37**
Adrian Cl. RG27: H Win 3K **13**
Aghemund Cl.
　RG24: Chin 5G **9**
Agricola Wlk. SP10: A'ver . . .3G **37**
Ajax Cl. RG24: Chin 4H **9**
Alanbrooke Cl.
　RG27: H Win 2J **13**
Albany Rd. SP10: A'ver 6D **36**
Albert Yd. RG21: B'toke 5D **16**
Albion Pl. RG27: H Win 2J **13**
Aldermaston Rd.
　RG24: Sher J 5K **7**
　RG26: M She 1K **7**

Aldermaston Rd. Rdbt.
　RG24: B'toke 1B **16**
Aldermaston Rd. Sth.
　RG21: B'toke 2B **16**
Alderney Av. RG22: B'toke . . .3H **23**
Alders Cl. RG21: B'toke 4F **17**
　　　　　　　　　(off Loddon Dr.)
Alderwood RG24: Chin 5H **9**
Alderwood Dr.
　RG27: Hoo 6B **12**
Aldrin Cl. SP10: Charl 3D **36**
Aldworth Cres.
　RG22: B'toke 5A **16**
Alencon Ho. RG21: B'toke . . .4D **16**
　　　　　　　　(off Alencon Wlk.)
Alencon Link RG21: B'toke . .4C **16**
Alexander Bell Cen.
　SP10: A'ver 5A **36**
Alexander Rd. RG25: Over . . .4D **32**

Alexandra Rd.
　RG21: B'toke 4B **16**
　SP10: A'ver 6E **36**
Alexandra Ter.
　RG27: Sher L 6G **5**
　RG29: N War 5C **20**
　　　　　　　　　　(off Bridge Rd.)
Alfred Gdns. SP10: A'ver . . .4E **36**
Allen Cl. RG21: B'toke 6B **16**
Allenmoor La. RG27: Roth . . .1J **11**
Alley La. RG25: Elli 7E **24**
Allington Ri. RG27: Sher L . . .3J **9**
Alliston Way RG22: B'toke . . .6H **15**
Allnutt Av. RG21: B'toke 4E **16**
Almerston Rd.
　RG24: Sher J 1K **7**
Almond Cl. RG24: Old B 3J **17**
Alpine Cl. RG22: B'toke 6G **15**

Black Dam Rdbt.—Charter Alley

Black Dam Rdbt. RG21: B'toke 5G 17
Black Dam Way RG21: B'toke 6F 17
Blackdown Cl. RG22: B'toke 6H 15
Blacksmiths Rdbt. SP10: A'ver 5G 37
Blackstocks La. RG27: Nat S, U Nat 4F 19
Black Swan Yd. *SP10: A'ver 6G 37*
(off East St.)
Blackthorn Way RG23: B'toke 3J 15
Blackwater Cl. RG21: B'toke 4E 16
RG23: Oak 1B 22
Blaegrove La. RG27: U Nat 5F 19
Blair Rd. RG21: B'toke 6C 16
Blake Cl. RG29: Odi 2C 28
Blakes Ct. SP10: A'ver 5F 37
Blendon Dr. SP10: A'ver 5C 36
Blenheim Rd. RG24: Old B 4A 18
Bliss Cl. RG22: B'toke 1A 24
Blossom Cl. SP10: A'ver 7B 36
Bloswood Dr. RG28: Whit 6B 30
Bloswood La. RG28: Hur P, Whit 3A 30
Bluebell Cl. SP10: A'ver 7B 36
Blueberry Gdns. SP10: A'ver 7B 36
Bluehaven Wlk. RG27: Hoo 7K 11
Blue Hayes Cl. SP10: A'ver 7F 37
Blunden Cl. RG21: B'toke 1C 24
Blunt Rd. RG22: B'toke 6F 23
Bodmin Cl. RG22: B'toke 6H 15
Bolton Cres. RG22: B'toke 6A 16
Bond Cl. RG24: B'toke 1G 17
Boon Way RG23: Oak 7A 14
Borden Gates SP10: A'ver 7F 37
Borkum Cl. SP10: A'ver 3E 36
Borodin Cl. RG22: B'toke 2B 24
Borough Ct. Rd. RG27: H Win 5E 12
Borsberry Cl. SP10: A'ver 6G 37
Boscowen Cl. *SP10: A'ver 6J 37*
(off London Rd.)
Bottle La. RG27: Matt 1A 12
Bounty Ri. RG21: B'toke 5C 16
Bounty Rd. RG21: B'toke 5C 16
Bourne Ct. RG21: B'toke 4F 17
SP10: A'ver 4H 37
(off River Way)
Bourne Fld. RG24: Sher J 4A 8
Bow Dr. RG27: Sher L 7G 5
Bow Fld. RG27: Hoo 7C 12
Bow Gdns. RG27: Sher L 7G 5
Bow Gro. RG27: Sher L 6G 5
Bowling Grn. Dr. RG27: Hoo 7K 11
Bowlplex
West Ham 4J 15
Bowman Rd. RG24: Chin 4H 9
Bowyer Cl. RG21: B'toke 5C 16
Boyce Cl. RG22: B'toke 2J 23
Bracher Cl. SP10: A'ver 6G 37
Bracken Bank RG24: Lych 1H 17
Brackenbury SP10: A'ver 5C 36
Brackens, The RG22: B'toke 4J 23
Brackley Av. RG27: H Win 2H 13
Brackley Way RG22: B'toke 1J 23
Bracknell La. RG27: H Win, Haze 1H 13
Bradbury Cl. RG28: Whit 6B 30
Bradman Sq. *SP10: A'ver 3H 37*
(off Cricketers Way)
Bradwell Cl. SP10: Charl 3C 36
Braemar Dr. RG23: Oak 7A 14
Brahms Rd. RG22: B'toke 2A 24
Braine L'Alleud Rd. RG21: B'toke 3D 16
Bramble Way RG24: Old B 3A 18
Brambling Cl. RG22: B'toke 3F 23
Bramblys Cl. RG21: B'toke 5C 16
Bramblys Dr. RG21: B'toke 5C 16
Bramdown Hgts. RG22: B'toke 4H 23
BRAMLEY 4C 4
BRAMLEY GREEN 5D 4
Bramley Grn. Rd. RG26: B'ley 5D 4
Bramley La. RG26: B'ley 3C 4
Bramley Rd. RG7: Sil 1A 4
RG26: B'ley 7A 4
RG27: Sher L 6G 5
Bramley Station (Rail) 4C 4
Brampton Gdns. RG22: B'toke 5H 23
Bramshott Dr. RG27: Hoo 7B 12
Brancaster Av. SP10: Charl 3C 36
Branton Cl. RG22: B'toke 6J 15
Breach La. RG27: Sher L 7H 5
Breadels Ct. RG22: B'toke 6H 23
Breadels Fld. RG22: B'toke 6G 23
Bremen Gdns. SP10: A'ver 4E 36
Brewer Cl. RG22: B'toke 6J 15
Brew Ho. La. RG27: H Win 2K 13
Brickfields Cl. RG24: Lych 1H 17
Bridge Rd. RG29: N War 5C 20
Bridge St. RG25: Over 3C 32
SP10: A'ver 7F 37
BRIGHTON HILL 2K 23
Brighton Hill Cen. RG22: B'toke 2K 23
Brighton Hill Pde. RG22: B'toke 2K 23
Brighton Hill Retail Pk. RG22: B'toke 7A 16
Brighton Hill Rdbt. RG22: B'toke 7A 16
Brighton Way RG22: B'toke 2K 23
Britannia Dr. RG22: B'toke 6G 23
Britten Rd. RG22: B'toke 1A 24
Broadhurst Gro. RG24: Lych 2H 17
Broad Leaze RG27: Hoo 6A 12
BROADMERE 6A 24
Broadmere RG25: Far W 7A 24
Broadmere Rd. RG22: B'toke 5G 23
BROAD OAK 5G 21
Broad Oak La. RG29: Odi 6G 21
Broad Wlk. RG25: B'toke 2G 25
Broadway RG28: Whit 7D 30
Broadway, The *SP10: A'ver 7F 37*
(off Western Rd.)
Brocas Dr. RG21: B'toke 2E 16
Bromelia Cl. RG26: B'ley 3C 4
Bronze Cl. RG22: B'toke 6G 23
Brooke Dr. SP10: A'ver 5D 36
Brookfield Cl. RG24: Chin 5J 9
Brooks Cl. RG28: Whit 7D 30
Brooks Ri. SP10: A'ver 5D 36
Brookvale Cl. RG21: B'toke 4C 16
Brookvale School RG21: B'toke 4B 16
Brookway SP11: Ann V 3B 38
Brown Cft. RG27: Hoo 7K 11
Browning Cl. RG24: B'toke 1E 16
Browns Cl. RG26: B'ley 3C 4
Brunel Ga. SP10: A'ver 4A 36
Brunel Rd. RG21: B'toke 3A 16
Brunswick Pl. RG21: B'toke 1B 24
Buckby La. RG21: B'toke 4F 17
Buckfast Cl. RG24: B'toke 7C 8
Buckingham Ct. RG22: B'toke 2G 23
Buckingham Pde. RG22: B'toke 1G 23
Buckland Av. RG22: B'toke 1K 23
Buckland Mill RG27: Hoo 1J 19
Buckland Pde. RG22: B'toke 7K 15
BUCKSKIN 6G 15
Buckskin La. RG22: B'toke 7G 15
Budd's Cl. RG21: B'toke 5C 16
Buffins Cnr. RG29: Odi 7C 20
Buffins Rd. RG29: Odi 7C 20
Bufton Fld. RG29: N War 6C 20
Bulls Bushes RG27: Hoo 1K 19
Bullsdown Cl. RG27: Sher L 6F 5
Bunnian Pl. RG21: B'toke 3D 16
Bunting M. RG22: B'toke 3F 23
Burberry Ho. RG27: Hoo 7A 12
Burdock Cl. SP11: G Cla 7E 38
Burgage Fld. RG28: Whit 5D 30
Burgate Cres. RG27: Sher L 3K 9
Burgess Cl. RG29: Odi 7C 20
Burgess Rd. RG21: B'toke 3C 16
Burkal Dr. SP10: A'ver 2F 37
Burley La. RG25: Ashe 6G 33
Burlingham Grange RG29: N War 6C 20
Burnaby Cl. RG22: B'toke 6J 15
Burnhams Cl. SP10: A'ver 3F 37
Burns Cl. RG24: B'toke 1E 16
Burrowfields RG22: B'toke 5H 23
Burton's Gdns. RG24: Old B 2K 17
BURY, THE 7E 20
Bury, The RG29: Odi 6E 20
Burydown Mead RG25: N Wal 2D 34
Buryfields RG29: Odi 7E 20
Bury Hill Cl. SP11: Ann V 3C 38
Bury Rd. RG23: B'toke 3K 15
Butler Cl. RG22: B'toke 5J 15
Buttermere Dr. RG22: B'toke 1G 23
Butts Mdw. RG27: Hoo 7A 12
Butty, The RG21: B'toke 4F 17
Byfleet Av. RG24: Old B 3K 17
Byng Wlk. SP10: A'ver 6J 37
Byrd Gdns. RG22: B'toke 3J 23
Byron Cl. RG24: B'toke 7F 9

C

Cadnam Cl. RG23: Oak 7B 14
Caerleon Dr. SP10: A'ver 2F 37
Caernarvon Cl. RG23: B'toke 4J 15
Caesar Cl. *RG23: B'toke 2J 15*
(off Wellington Ter.)
SP10: A'ver 3G 37
Caesar's Way RG28: Whit 5B 30
Cairngorm Cl. RG22: B'toke 5H 15
Caithness Cl. RG23: Oak 1A 22
Calder Ct. SP10: A'ver 4H 37
Calleva Cl. RG22: B'toke 3H 23
Camberry Cl. RG21: B'toke 6E 16
Cambrian Way RG22: B'toke 6H 15
Camelot Cl. SP10: A'ver 4F 37
Camfield Cl. RG21: B'toke 6E 16
Camford Cl. RG22: B'toke 6G 23
Camlea Cl. RG21: B'toke 6E 16
Campbell Ct. RG26: B'ley 5E 4
Campbell Rd. RG26: B'ley 5E 4
Campion Way RG27: H Win 1K 13
Campsie Cl. RG22: B'toke 5H 15
Camrose Way RG21: B'toke 7E 16
Cam Wlk. RG21: B'toke 4F 17
Camwood Cl. RG21: B'toke 6E 16
Canadian Way RG24: B'toke 1J 15
Canal Cl. RG29: N War 5C 20
Canal Reach RG27: A'ell 4D 18
Canberra Way RG22: B'toke 6G 23
Candover Ct. RG22: B'toke 5F 23
Cannock Ct. RG22: B'toke 5J 15
Canterbury Cl. RG22: B'toke 2H 23
Carbonel Cl. RG23: Wort 4G 15
Cardinal M. SP10: A'ver 6F 37
Carisbrooke Cl. RG23: B'toke 3J 15
Carleton Cl. RG27: Hoo 7K 11
Carlisle Cl. RG23: B'toke 3J 15
Carmichael Way RG22: B'toke 2J 23
Carpenters Cl. RG27: Sher L 6G 5
Carpenters Ct. RG22: B'toke 7K 15
Carpenter's Down RG24: B'toke 7D 8
Cartel Bus Cen. RG24: B'toke 1G 17
Carters Mdw. SP10: Charl 4C 36
Castle Ri. RG29: N War 5C 20
Castle Rd. RG21: B'toke 6D 16
Castle Sq. RG21: B'toke 4D 16
Caston's Wlk. RG21: B'toke 5D 16
Caston's Yd. RG21: B'toke 5D 16
Catkin Cl. RG24: Chin 5H 9
Cattle La. SP11: Abb A 3A 38
Causeway Cotts. RG27: H Win 2K 13
Causton Rd. RG22: B'toke 6H 23
Cavalier Cl. RG24: Old B 3A 18
Cavalier Rd. RG24: Old B 3A 18
Cavel Ct. RG24: Lych 1J 17
Caxton Cl. SP10: A'ver 5B 36
Cayman Cl. RG24: B'toke 7F 9
Cedar Ter. RG27: H Win 3H 13
Cedar Tree Cl. RG23: Oak 2A 22
Cedar Wlk. SP10: A'ver 7C 36
Cedar Way RG23: B'toke 2K 15
Cedarwood RG24: Chin 5F 9
Celtic Dr. SP10: A'ver 1D 38
Cemetery Hill RG29: Odi 7E 20
Cemetery La. RG25: Up G 5F 27
Central Way SP10: A'ver 5K 37
Centre Court Tennis Cen. 7H 9
Centre Dr. RG24: Chin 7H 9
Centurion Way RG22: B'toke 3H 23
(not continuous)
Century Cl. RG25: Clid 3C 24
Chaffers Cl. RG29: L Sut 7D 28
Chaffinch Cl. RG22: B'toke 2G 23
Chaldon Grn. RG24: Lych 1J 17
Chalk Va. RG24: Old B 4A 18
Chalky Copse RG27: Hoo 6A 12
Challis Cl. RG22: B'toke 7J 15
Challoner Cl. RG22: B'toke 6J 15
Chandler Rd. RG21: B'toke 7C 16
Chantry Cen., The SP10: A'ver 6F 37
Chantry Cl. RG27: Hoo 1A 20
Chantry M. RG22: B'toke 3H 23
Chantry St. SP10: A'ver 6F 37
Chapel Cl. RG24: Old B 2K 17
RG25: Dumm 2H 35
Chapel Hill RG21: B'toke 3C 16
Chapel Pond Dr. RG29: N War 6C 20
Chapel River Cl. SP10: A'ver 7D 36
Chapel Row RG27: H Win 1K 13
Chapel St. RG25: N Wal 2C 34
Chapel Wlk. RG25: Clid 3C 24
Chapter Ter. RG27: H Win 1K 13
Charlcot Farm RG28: Whit 7C 30
Charledown Cl. RG25: Over 4C 32
Charledown Rd. RG25: Over 4C 32
Charles Cl. RG27: Hoo 7A 12
Charles Dalton Ct. SP10: A'ver 7F 37
Charles Richards Cl. RG21: B'toke 6C 16
Charles St. RG22: B'toke 5K 15
Charlotte Cl. SP10: A'ver 6J 37
CHARLTON 4D 36
Charlton Pl. SP10: A'ver 5F 37
Charlton Rd. SP10: A'ver 4D 36
(not continuous)
Charlton Rdbt. SP10: A'ver 4D 36
Charlton Sports & Leisure Cen. 3B 36
Charnwood Cl. RG22: B'toke 6H 15
SP10: A'ver 1G 39
CHARTER ALLEY 1F 7

Chatsworth Dr.
SP10: A'ver 7D 36
Chatsworth Grn.
RG22: B'toke 4J 23
Chatter La. RG28: Whit 6C 30
Chaucer Av. SP10: A'ver . . .5C 36
Chaucer Cl. RG24: B'toke . . .7E 8
Cheavley Cl. SP10: A'ver . . .6B 36
Chelmer Ct. RG21: B'toke . . .4F 17
(off Loddon Dr.)
Chelsea Ho. RG21: B'toke . . .4D 16
(off Festival Pl.)
Chequers Rd.
RG21: B'toke 4E 16
Cherry Cl. RG27: Hoo 6B 12
Cherry Orchard
RG28: B'toke 7D 30
SP10: A'ver 6E 36
Cherry Tree Rd.
SP10: A'ver 5D 36
Cherry Tree Wlk.
RG21: B'toke 1E 16
Cherrywood RG24: Chin 5G 9
Chesterfield Rd.
RG21: B'toke 6E 16
Chester Pl. RG21: B'toke . . .5C 16
Chestnut Av. SP10: A'ver . . .2E 38
Chestnut Bank
RG24: Old B 2K 17
Cheviot Cl. RG22: B'toke . . .6H 15
Chichester Cl. SP10: A'ver . . .6C 36
Chichester Pl.
RG22: B'toke 7A 16
Chiltern Way RG22: B'toke . . .6G 15
Chilton Ridge
RG22: B'toke 5H 23
CHINEHAM 6H 9
Chineham Bus. Pk.
RG24: Chin 4G 9
Chineham District Cen.
RG24: Chin 7H 9
Chineham La.
RG24: B'toke 1E 16
RG24: B'toke, Sher J 6B 8
Chineham Pk. Ct.
RG24: B'toke 1F 17
Chineham Shop. Cen.
RG24: Chin 7H 9
Chivers Cl. RG22: B'toke . . .6H 15
Chopin Rd. RG22: B'toke . . .2K 23
Church Cl. SP10: A'ver 6G 37
CHURCH END 2A 10
Church Farm Cl.
RG25: N Wal 1C 34
Churchill Av. RG29: Odi 1D 28
Churchill Cl.
RG27: H Win 1H 13
RG29: Odi 2D 28
Churchill Plaza
RG21: B'toke 4E 16
Churchill Way
RG21: B'toke 4D 16
SP10: A'ver 5G 37
Churchill Way E.
RG21: B'toke 4E 16
Churchill Way W.
RG21: B'toke 4A 16
RG22: B'toke 4A 16
SP10: A'ver 5B 36
Church Lands RG26: B'ley . . .4A 4
Church La. RG21: B'toke . . .4D 16
RG23: Wort 5G 15
RG24: Old B 3K 17
RG25: Clid 3C 24
RG27: H Win 4K 13
SP11: G Cla 6F 39
SP11: Up C 4E 38
Church M. SP11: Ann V 3B 38
Church Path RG24: Sher J . . .4A 8
RG27: Hoo 1K 19
RG27: Newn 7G 11
Church Rd. RG25: N Wal . . .2C 34
RG25: Over 3C 32
Church Sq. RG21: B'toke . . .4D 16
Church St. RG21: B'toke . . .4D 16
(not continuous)
RG25: Up G 5F 27
RG28: Whit 7B 30
RG29: Odi 6D 20
(not continuous)

Church Vw. RG27: H Win . . .4J 13
RG27: Hoo 7B 12
RG29: S War 7K 27
SP11: Up C 3D 38
Churn Cl. RG21: B'toke 2K 17
Chute Cl. RG26: B'ley 3C 4
Chute Ho. RG21: B'toke 4D 16
(off Church St.)
Cibbons Rd. RG24: Chin 5H 9
City Wall Ho. RG21: B'toke . .3F 17
Clappers Farm Rd.
RG7: Sil 1A 4
Clarendon Av. SP10: A'ver . . .1D 38
Clark M. RG28: Whit 7C 30
(off Church St.)
Clatford Mnr. SP11: Up C . . .3D 38
Claudius Cl. SP10: A'ver . . .2G 37
Claudius Dr. RG23: B'toke . . .2J 15
Claythorpe Rd.
RG22: B'toke 6J 15
Clayton Cl. RG27: H Win 3J 13
Cleaver Rd. RG22: B'toke . . .6J 15
Cleeve Rd. RG24: Sher J 6D 8
Clemence Gdns.
RG28: Whit 6C 30
Clere Gdns. RG24: Chin 6H 9
Clevedge Way
RG29: N War 5C 20
Cleveland Cl.
RG22: B'toke 6H 15
Cleves La. RG25: Up G 4F 27
CLIDDESDEN 3C 24
Cliddesden Ct.
RG21: B'toke 7D 16
Cliddesden La.
RG22: B'toke 5H 23
Cliddesden Rd.
RG21: B'toke 7D 16
Clifton Ter. RG21: B'toke . . .3D 16
Clifton Wlk. RG21: B'toke . . .4D 16
(off Festival Pl.)
Cloisters, The SP10: A'ver . . .6F 37
Close, The RG23: B'toke . . .2K 15
RG26: M She 2H 7
RG29: Odi 7D 20
Clover Fld. RG24: Lych 2H 17
Clover Leaf Way
RG24: Old B 5K 17
Clover M. SP10: A'ver 7G 37
Clyde Ct. SP10: A'ver 4H 37
Coachways SP10: A'ver 1F 39
Coates Cl. RG22: B'toke 1B 24
Cobbett Grn. RG22: B'toke . . .7A 16
Coldharbour RG25: N Wal . . .2C 34
Cold Harbour Cotts.
RG25: Clid 3B 24
Cold Harbour Ct.
SP10: A'ver 7G 37
Colebrook Way
SP10: A'ver 7C 36
Cole Cl. SP10: A'ver 2F 37
COLE HENLEY 1D 30
Coleman Cl. RG21: B'toke . . .2E 16
Colenzo Dr. SP10: A'ver 5G 37
College M. SP10: A'ver 6F 37
College Rd. RG21: B'toke . . .4B 16
Collingwood Wlk.
SP10: A'ver 6J 37
Collins Cl. SP10: Charl 3D 36
Colne Way RG21: B'toke 4F 17
COLT HILL 5F 21
Coltsfoot Pl. RG27: Hoo 6C 12
Columbine Rd.
RG22: B'toke 3G 23
Columbus Way
SP10: A'ver 5K 37
Colvin Cl. SP10: A'ver 7G 37
Colyer Cl. RG22: B'toke 6J 15
Compass Fld. RG27: Hoo . . .7B 12
Compton Cl. RG27: Hoo 7B 12
Compton Sq. SP10: A'ver . . .3H 37
Compton Way RG27: Sher L . .3K 9
Conholt Rd. SP10: A'ver 2F 39
Coniston Rd. RG22: B'toke . .1G 23
Constable Cl.
RG21: B'toke 6F 17
Constable Ct. SP10: A'ver . . .5F 37
Constantine Sq.
SP10: A'ver 3H 37
(off Cricketers Way)

Constantine Way
RG22: B'toke 4G 23
Coombehurst Dr.
RG21: B'toke 7D 16
Coopers Cl. RG26: B'ley 4C 4
Coopers La. RG26: B'ley 4B 4
Coop La. RG27: A'ell 3E 18
Copland Cl. RG22: B'toke . . .2J 23
Coppice M. RG23: B'toke . . .3J 15
Coppice Pale RG24: Old B . . .6J 9
Copse, The RG23: Dumm . . .7D 22
Copse Cvn. Site, The
RG23: Dumm 7D 22
Copse Fld. RG24: Lych 1J 17
Copse La. RG29: L Sut 7D 28
Copse Rd. RG25: Over 1D 32
Copse Vw. Cl. RG24: Chin . . .5H 9
Cordale Rd. RG21: B'toke . . .6C 16
Corelli Rd. RG22: B'toke 2B 24
Corfe Wlk. RG23: B'toke 3J 15
Corinthian Cl.
RG22: B'toke 3H 23
SP10: A'ver 2G 37
Cormorant Cl.
RG22: B'toke 2F 23
Cornfields SP10: A'ver 1H 39
Cornfields, The
RG22: B'toke 3J 23
Cornish Cl. RG22: B'toke 6J 15
Coronation Cl. RG29: Odi . . .6E 20
Coronation Cotts.
RG23: W Law 2E 14
Coronation Rd.
RG21: B'toke 3E 16
Corunna Main SP10: A'ver . . .6G 37
Cotswold Cl. RG22: B'toke . . .5H 15
Cottage Grn. RG27: H Win . . .3K 13
SP11: G Cla 7E 38
Cottle Cl. RG21: B'toke 7C 16
Council Rd. RG21: B'toke . . .5D 16
COUNTESS OF BRECKNOCK
HOUSE (HOSPICE) 5D 36
Court Drove RG25: B'toke . . .1B 32
Courtyard, The
RG22: B'toke 5G 23
Coventry Cl. RG22: B'toke . . .2H 23
Cowdery Hgts.
RG24: Old B 3G 17
COW DOWN 3K 39
Cowdown La.
SP11: A'ver, G Cla 4G 39
Cowdrey Sq. SP10: A'ver . . .3G 37
Cowfold La.
RG27: Matt, Roth 2A 12
Cowslad Dr. RG24: Old B 6J 9
Cowslip Bank RG24: Lych . . .1H 17
Crabtree Way RG24: Old B . . .5K 17
Crawts Rd. RG25: Over 4C 32
Crescent, The
RG24: B'toke 1K 15
RG26: B'ley 4B 4
(off Oakmead)
SP10: A'ver 1F 39
SP11: G Cla 6E 38
SP11: Up C 3D 38
Cress Gdns. SP10: A'ver 1E 38
Creswell RG27: Hoo 7D 12
Cricketers Way
SP10: A'ver 3G 37
Cricket Grn. RG27: H Win . . .2K 13
Cricket Grn. La.
RG27: H Win 2K 13
Cricklade Pl. SP10: A'ver . . .5D 36
Crockford La.
RG24: B'toke, Chin 7F 9
(not continuous)
Croft Av. SP10: A'ver 1F 39
Crofters Mdw. RG24: Lych . . .1H 17
Croft Gdns. SP10: A'ver 1F 39
Crofton Sq. RG27: Sher L . . .3J 9
Croft Rd. RG23: Oak 7A 14
RG27: H Win 4H 13

Crofts, The RG22: B'toke 4J 23
Cromwell Cl. RG24: Old B . . .3K 17
Cromwell Rd.
RG21: B'toke 3C 16
Cropmark Way
RG21: B'toke 3H 23
Crossborough Gdns.
RG21: B'toke 5E 16
Crossborough Hill
RG21: B'toke 5E 16
Cross La. SP10: A'ver 6E 36
Cross St. RG21: B'toke 5D 16
Crossways RG28: Whit 5C 30
Crossways, The
SP10: A'ver 5E 36
Crown Cres. RG24: Old B . . .3J 17
Crownfields RG29: Odi 7D 20
Crown Hgts. RG21: B'toke . . .4D 16
Crown La. RG24: Old B 3J 17
RG27: Nat S, Newn 2F 19
Crown Way SP10: A'ver 5J 37
Croye Cl. SP10: A'ver 6E 36
Cuckoo Cl. RG25: N Wal 2C 34
(not continuous)
Cuckoo Leaze RG26: Cha A . . .1F 7
CUFAUDE 1F 9
Cufaude La. RG24: Chin 4H 9
RG26: B'ley 6A 4
Cuffelle Cl. RG24: Chin 5J 9
Culver Rd. RG21: B'toke 6C 16
Cumberland Av.
RG22: B'toke 1A 24
Cummins Cl. SP10: A'ver 7H 37
Curlew Cl. RG22: B'toke 1G 23
Cusden Dr. SP10: A'ver 4F 37
Cuxhaven Way SP10: A'ver . . .3E 36
Cypress Gro. SP10: A'ver . . .7B 36
Cyprus Rd. RG22: B'toke 5J 23

D

Dacre Cl. SP10: Charl 3C 36
Daffodil Cl. RG22: B'toke . . .2G 23
Dahlia Cl. RG22: B'toke 2H 23
Dahlia Cl. SP10: A'ver 1C 38
Dairy Wlk. RG27: H Win 2K 13
Dalewood RG22: B'toke 7G 15
Damsel Path RG21: B'toke . . .4F 17
Dancers Mdw.
RG24: Sher J 5B 8
Dances Cl. SP10: A'ver 5G 37
Dance's La. RG28: Whit 5C 30
Danebury Rd.
RG22: B'toke 4H 23
Danegeld Cl. SP10: A'ver . . .2G 37
Danehurst Pl. SP10: A'ver . . .6B 36
Danes, The RG21: B'toke 4E 16
DANESHILL 1F 17
Daneshill Ct. RG24: Lych 7H 9
Daneshill Dr. RG24: Lych 1H 17
Daneshill E. Ind. Est.
RG24: B'toke 2G 17
Daneshill Ind. Est.
RG24: B'toke 2G 17
Daneshill Rdbt.
RG24: B'toke 2G 17
Daneshill W. Ind. Est.
RG24: B'toke 1F 17
Daniel Rd. RG28: Whit 7D 30
Dankworth Rd.
RG22: B'toke 2J 23
(not continuous)
Darcy Cl. RG21: B'toke 2E 16
D'arcy Ho. RG22: B'toke 7J 15
Darent Ct. RG21: B'toke 4F 17
(off Loddon Dr.)
Dark La. RG24: Sher J 5A 8
Darlington Rd.
RG21: B'toke 3C 16
Dartmouth Wlk.
RG22: B'toke 6J 15
Dartmouth Way
RG22: B'toke 6J 15
Davenport Ga. SP10: A'ver . . .5B 36
Davy Cl. RG22: B'toke 5A 16
DEANE 2K 33
Deane Cotts. RG25: Dea 2K 33
Deanes Cl. RG21: B'toke 3E 16
Deep La. RG21: B'toke 4H 16

Deerfield Cl. RG26: B'ley 5E 4
Deer Pk. Vw. RG29: Odi 6E 20
De La Rue Ho.
   RG21: B'toke 3F 17
Delibes Rd. RG22: B'toke 2B 24
Delius Cl. RG22: B'toke 1A 24
Dell, The RG24: Old B 4A 18
Dellands RG25: Over 4C 32
Dellands La. RG25: Over 4B 32
Dellfield RG23: Oak 6B 14
Dell Rd. SP10: A'ver 5E 36
Dene Ct. SP10: A'ver 7G 37
Dene Path SP10: A'ver 7G 37
Dene Rd. SP10: A'ver 7G 37
Denham Dr. RG22: B'toke . . .7J 15
Denning Mead SP10: A'ver . .7E 36
Denvale Trade Pk.
   RG21: B'toke 2B 16
De Port Gdns. RG24: Old B . . .6J 9
Deptford La. RG29: Grey 6K 19
Derbyfields RG29: N War 3C 20
Derwent Rd. RG22: B'toke . . .1G 23
Dever Way RG23: Oak 1B 22
Devonshire Bus. Pk.
   RG21: B'toke 2B 16
Devonshire Pl.
   RG21: B'toke 5C 16
Dewpond Wlk. RG24: Lych . .1H 17
Dexter Sq. SP10: A'ver 3H 37
Diana Cl. RG22: B'toke 6A 16
Dibley Cl. RG22: B'toke 6J 15
Dicken's La. RG24: Old B . . .5J 17
   RG25: Tun 7H 17
Dilly La. RG27: H Win 4J 13
Dinwoodie Dr.
   RG24: B'toke 1A 16
DIPLEY **1E 12**
Dipley Rd.
   RG27: H Win, Matt 1C 12
Dixon Rd. RG26: B'ley 6D 4
Doctors Acre RG27: Hoo 6D 12
Dollis Grn. RG26: B'ley 4C 4
Dominica Cl. RG24: B'toke . . .6E 8
Domitian Gdns.
   RG24: B'toke 1J 15
Dorchester Cl.
   RG23: B'toke 4H 15
Dorchester Rd. RG27: Hoo . .7A 12
Dorchester Way
   RG29: Grey 5A 20
Dorrel Cl. RG22: B'toke 4H 23
Doswell Way RG21: B'toke . . .3E 16
Doughty Way SP10: A'ver . . .5K 37
Douglas Rd. SP11: A'ver 6A 36
Dove Cl. RG22: B'toke 1F 23
   SP10: A'ver 4G 37
Dover Cl. RG23: B'toke 3K 15
Down La. RG25: Mapl 6D 18
Downsland Ct.
   RG21: B'toke *5B 16*
   (off Downsland Pde.)
Downsland Pde.
   RG21: B'toke 5B 16
Downsland Rd.
   RG21: B'toke 5B 16
   (not continuous)
Down St. RG25: Dumm 2H 35
Dragonfly Dr. RG24: Lych . . .1H 17
Drake Cl. SP10: A'ver 5J 37
Driftway Rd. RG27: Hoo 7C 12
Drive, The RG23: Oak 1B 22
Drove, The SP10: A'ver 6C 36
Dryden Cl. RG24: B'toke 7E 8
Duddon Way RG21: B'toke . . .4F 17
Dudley Cl. RG23: B'toke 4H 15
Duke Cl. SP10: A'ver 5J 37
DUMMER **2H 35**
DUMMER CLUMP **2K 35**
Dummer Down La.
   RG25: Dumm 4F 35
Duncan Ct. SP10: A'ver 6J 37
Dundee Gdns.
   RG22: B'toke 5H 15
Dunley's Hill
   RG29: N War, Odi 6C 20
Dunmow Rd. SP10: A'ver . . .1G 39
Dunsford Cres.
   RG21: B'toke 2J 15
Durham Way RG22: B'toke . .2H 23
Durley Cl. SP10: A'ver 7D 36

E

Eagle Cl. RG22: B'toke 2F 23
Eagle Cl. RG24: B'toke 3H 17
Eardley Av. SP10: A'ver 5C 36
Eastfield Av. RG21: B'toke . . .4E 16
Eastfield Cl. SP10: A'ver 6H 37
Eastfield Lodge
   SP10: A'ver *6G 37*
   (off Eastfield Rd.)
Eastfield Rd. SP10: A'ver 6G 37
EAST OAKLEY **1B 22**
East Portway SP10: A'ver 6B 36
EASTROP **5F 17**
Eastrop La. RG21: B'toke 4E 16
Eastrop Rdbt.
   RG21: B'toke 4E 16
Eastrop Way
   RG21: B'toke 4E 16
East St. SP10: A'ver 6G 37
Edgar Cl. SP10: A'ver 2G 37
Edgehill Cl. RG22: B'toke 6H 15
Edison Rd. RG21: B'toke 2A 16
Edrich Sq. SP10: A'ver 4G 37
Elbe Way SP10: A'ver 3E 36
Elbow Cnr. RG21: B'toke 4D 16
Elderberry Bank
   RG24: Lych 1H 17
Elder Cres. SP10: A'ver 1C 38
Elder Ho. RG24: Old B 4B 18
Elder Rd. RG24: B'toke 1K 15
Elgar Cl. RG22: B'toke 2A 24
Elizabethan Ri.
   RG25: N Wal 1C 34
Elizabeth Rd.
   RG22: B'toke 6A 16
Ellen Gdns. RG26: B'ley 4B 4
Ellington Cl. SP11: A'ver 7A 36
Ellington Dr. RG22: B'toke . . .3J 23
Elm Bank Rd. SP10: A'ver . . .1F 39
Elm Rd. RG24: Sher J 6K 7
   RG25: Over 1D 32
Elms, The SP10: A'ver 7E 36
Elms Rd. RG27: Hoo 6A 12
Elmwood RG24: Chin 5G 9
Elmwood Pde.
   RG23: B'toke 2J 15
Elmwood Way
   RG23: B'toke 2J 15
Elvetham Ri. RG24: Old B . . .7J 9
Emden Rd. SP10: A'ver 3E 36
Englefield Way
   RG24: Sher J 6D 8
English Wood
   RG24: B'toke 2J 15
Enham Arch Rdbt.
   SP10: A'ver 4G 37
Enham La.
   SP10: A'ver, K Enh, Charl
   .3D 36
Ennerdale Cl.
   RG22: B'toke 7H 15
Enterprise Ct.
   RG24: B'toke 2F 17
Esher Cl. RG22: B'toke 1K 23
Essex Rd. RG21: B'toke 4C 16
Ethelbert Dr. SP10: Charl . . .3C 36
Eton Cl. RG22: B'toke 4G 23
Europa Cl. RG26: B'ley 4C 4
Euskirchen Way
   RG22: B'toke 4J 15
Eversfield Cl. SP10: A'ver 6E 36
Evesham Wlk.
   RG24: B'toke 7D 8
Evingar Gdns. RG28: Whit . . .5C 30
Evingar Rd. RG28: Whit 6C 30
Ewhurst Rd. RG26: Rams 4A 6
Exbury Way SP10: A'ver 7D 36
Exeter Cl. RG22: B'toke 3H 23
Exmoor Cl. RG21: B'toke 6H 15

F

Fabian Cl. RG21: B'toke 5C 16
Fair Cl. RG28: Whit 7B 30
   (not continuous)

Fairclose Ter. *RG28: Whit* . .*6C 30*
   (off Fair Cl.)
Fairfield RG28: Whit 5C 30
Fairfields Arts Cen. **5D 16**
Fairfields Rd.
   RG21: B'toke 6D 16
Fairholme Pde.
   RG27: Hoo 7A 12
FAIR OAK GREEN **1E 4**
Fair Oak La. RG7: Stra S 1E 4
Fairthorne Ho.
   RG22: B'toke 6A 16
Fairthorne Ri.
   RG24: Old B 4A 18
Fairview Mdw. RG23: Oak . . .2B 22
Falcon Cl. RG22: B'toke 1F 23
Falkland Rd. RG24: B'toke . . .6E 8
Fanum Ho. RG21: B'toke 3F 17
Faraday Ct. RG24: B'toke 1F 17
Faraday Office Pk.
   RG24: B'toke 1F 17
Faraday Pk. SP10: A'ver 5A 36
Faraday Rd. RG24: B'toke . . .1F 17
Farleigh La.
   RG25: Dumm . . . .
   . . . . .2H 35 & 7H 23
Farleigh Ri. RG21: B'toke . . .7E 16
Farleigh Rd. RG25: Clid 3C 24
   RG25: Clid, Far W 7K 23
FARLEIGH WALLOP **7A 24**
Farm Cotts. RG24: B'toke . . .1K 15
Farm Ground Cl.
   RG27: Hoo 7C 12
Farm Rd. SP11: A'ver 1A 38
Farm Vw. Dr. RG24: Chin . . .5J 9
Farnham Rd. RG29: Odi 6E 20
Faroe Cl. RG24: B'toke 7F 9
Farriers Cl. RG26: B'ley 4C 4
Farrs Av. SP10: A'ver 1G 39
Fayrewood Chase
   RG22: B'toke 3H 23
Feathers La. RG21: B'toke . . .5D 16
Feathers Yd. RG21: B'toke . . .5D 16
Felders Mede RG27: Hoo . . .7D 12
Feld Way RG24: Lych 1J 17
Fencott Pl. RG21: B'toke 3D 16
Fennel Cl. RG24: Chin 4J 9
Ferguson Cl. RG21: B'toke . . .7D 16
Ferndale Gdns.
   RG27: Hoo 6A 12
Ferndale Rd. SP10: A'ver 5D 36
Ferndown Cl.
   RG22: B'toke 6G 23
Fernhill Pl. RG27: Sher L 3K 9
Ferrell Fld. RG27: Hoo 7K 11
Festival Pl. RG21: B'toke 4D 16
Fingle Dr. SP10: A'ver 6D 36
Finkley Down Farm Pk. . . .**3K 37**
Finkley Rd. SP11: Sman 2J 37
Firecrest Rd. RG22: B'toke . . .3F 23
Firs, The SP10: A'ver 6D 36
Firs La. RG29: Odi 7C 20
Firs Way RG23: B'toke 1C 22
Firsway RG28: Whit 6C 30
Fisher Cl. SP10: A'ver 6J 37
Fiske Cl. RG22: B'toke 5J 15
Flaxfield Ct. RG21: B'toke . . .4C 16
Flaxfield Rd. RG21: B'toke . . .4C 16
Fleet Rd. RG27: H Win 2K 13
Flensburg Cl. SP10: A'ver . . .3E 36
Fletcher Cl. RG21: B'toke . . .5B 16
Flinders Cl. SP10: A'ver 5K 37
Flint Cl. SP10: A'ver 1D 38
Floral Way SP10: A'ver 1C 38
Florence Cl. SP10: A'ver 3G 37
   (not continuous)
Florence Portal Cl.
   RG28: Lave 6J 31
Florence Way
   RG24: B'toke 1J 15
Flowerdew Ct. SP10: A'ver . .1G 39
Focus 303 Bus. Cen.
   SP10: A'ver 5K 37
Focus Way SP10: A'ver 5J 37
Folly La. RG7: Stra S 4E 4
   RG26: B'ley 4E 4
Folly Roundabout, The
   SP10: A'ver 5E 36
Ford La. RG25: Up G 3K 27
   RG29: S War 3K 27

Forefield Dr. RG22: B'toke . . .5G 23
Forest Dr. RG24: Chin 4H 9
Forge Cl. RG26: B'ley 5D 4
Forge Fld. SP10: A'ver 5G 37
Forsythia Wlk.
   RG21: B'toke 1E 16
Fort Hill Dr. RG23: B'toke . . .3J 15
Forum Cl. RG23: B'toke 4H 15
Fosters Bus. Pk.
   RG27: Hoo 1J 19
Foundry Cl. RG27: Hoo 7A 12
Foundry Rd. SP11: Ann V . . .3B 38
Fountains Cl. RG24: B'toke . . .7C 8
Fountain's Mall RG29: Odi . . .6E 20
Four Acre Coppice
   RG27: Hoo 6C 12
Four Lanes Cl. RG24: Chin . . .5J 9
FOXCOTTE **3B 36**
Foxcotte Cl. SP10: Charl 4C 36
Foxcotte La. SP10: Charl 3B 36
   SP11: Charl 3B 36
Foxcotte Rd. SP10: Charl . . .3A 36
FOXDOWN **1D 32**
Foxdown RG25: Over 1D 32
Foxglove Cl. RG22: B'toke . . .3G 23
FOXHALL **7J 23**
Fox La. RG23: Oak 7C 14
Foxmoor Cl. RG23: Oak 6B 14
Fox's Furlong RG24: Chin . . .4K 9
Foyle Pl. RG21: B'toke 7C 16
Frances Rd. RG21: B'toke . . .5C 16
Franklin Av. RG27: H Win . . .1J 13
Fraser Cl. RG24: Old B 3K 17
FREEFOLK **5G 31**
Freefolk Priors RG28: Free . .5G 31
Freemantle Cl.
   RG21: B'toke 2F 17
Frescade Cres.
   RG21: B'toke 6C 16
Frithmead Cl.
   RG21: B'toke 7C 16
Frog La. RG25: Mapl 4D 18
   RG27: Roth 1H 11
Frome Cl. RG21: B'toke 4F 17
   RG23: Oak 1C 22
Frouds Cl. RG27: Hoo 1K 19
Froyle La. RG29: S War 7A 28
Fry Sq. SP10: A'ver 4G 37
   (off Cricketers Way)
Fulbrook Way RG29: Odi 2D 28
Fulham Ho. *RG21: B'toke* . . .*4D 16*
   (off Festival Pl.)
Fullerton Rd.
   SP11: Red R, G Cla 6A 38
Fulmar Cl. RG22: B'toke 3F 23
Fuzzy Drove RG22: B'toke . . .2F 23
Fylingdales Cl.
   RG22: B'toke 5H 15

G

Gage Cl. RG24: Lych 2H 17
Gaiger Av. RG27: Sher L 3K 9
Gainsborough Ct.
   SP10: A'ver 5E 36
Gainsborough Rd.
   RG21: B'toke 7E 16
Gala Bingo
   West Ham **4K 15**
Galahad Cl. SP10: A'ver 4F 37
Gales Cl. SP10: A'ver 6F 37
Galileo Pk. SP10: A'ver 5B 36
Gallaghers Mead
   SP10: A'ver 6B 36
Galloway Cl. RG22: B'toke . . .6H 15
Gander Dr. RG24: B'toke 1J 15
Gannet Cl. RG22: B'toke 2F 23
Garden Cl. RG27: Hoo 7K 11
   SP10: A'ver 7G 37
Gaston La. RG29: S War 4K 27
Gaston's Wood Ind. Est.
   RG24: Chin 7F 9
Gateway Ho. RG21: B'toke . . .3F 17
Gawaine Cl. SP10: A'ver 4F 37
Geffery's Flds.
   RG21: B'toke 5E 16
Geffery's Ho. RG27: Hoo 6B 12
Genoa Ct. SP10: A'ver 2G 37
   (not continuous)

George St.—Holly Dr.

George St. RG21: B'toke 4B 16
George Yd. SP10: A'ver 7G 37
Georgia Cl. SP10: A'ver 1C 38
German Rd. RG26: B'ley 5D 4
Gershwin Ct. RG22: B'toke . . .2J 23
Gershwin Rd.
RG22: B'toke 2J 23
Gilbard Ct. RG24: Chin 5J 9
Gilbert Cl. RG24: B'toke 7E 8
Gilberts Mead Cl.
SP11: Ann V 3B 38
Gillies Dr. RG24: B'toke 1J 15
Glade Cl. RG24: Chin 6H 9
Glamis Cl. RG23: Oak 7B 14
Glastonbury Cl.
RG24: B'toke 1C 16
Glebe Cl. RG25: Dumm 2H 35
Glebe Ho. *RG21: B'toke 3D 16*
(off Vyne Rd.)
Glebelands SP11: G Cla 6G 39
Glebe La. RG23: Wort 5G 15
RG27: H Win 3K 13
Glebe Mdw. RG25: Over 3C 32
Glen Cl. SP10: A'ver 6D 36
Gleneagles Cl.
RG22: B'toke 5G 23
Glenmore Bus. Pk.
SP10: A'ver 7C 36
Gloucester Dr.
RG22: B'toke 2H 23
Goat La. RG21: B'toke 4E 16
Goch Way
SP10: A'ver, Charl 4D 36
Goddards Cl. RG27: Sher L . . .7G 5
Goddards Firs RG23: Oak 2C 22
Goddards La. RG27: Sher L . . .7F 5
Goddards Mead
SP10: A'ver 7D 36
Goddard Sq. *SP10: A'ver 4H 37*
(off Cricketers Way)
Golden Lion Rdbt.
RG21: B'toke 7D 16
Goldfinch Gdns.
RG22: B'toke 4F 23
Goodman Cl. RG21: B'toke . . .5B 16
GOODWORTH CLATFORD . . .6F 39
Goodworth Vw.
SP11: G Cla 6F 39
Goose Grn. RG27: Hoo 6K 11
Goose La. RG27: Hoo 6A 12
Gordon Cl. RG21: B'toke 3E 16
Gower Cl. RG21: B'toke 2D 16
Gower Cres. RG27: Hoo 7B 12
Gracemere Cres.
RG22: B'toke 3F 23
Grace Sq. SP10: A'ver 4H 37
Grafton Way RG22: B'toke . . .5K 15
Grainger Cl. RG22: B'toke . . .1A 24
Grampian Way
RG22: B'toke 6H 15
Granada Pl. SP10: A'ver 5H 37
Grange La. RG27: H Win 2H 13
Graveney Sq. *SP10: A'ver . . .4G 37*
(off Cricketers Way)
Gt. Binfields Cres.
RG24: Lych 1H 17
Gt. Binfields Rd.
RG24: Chin, Lych 7H 9
Gt. Marlow RG27: Hoo 7D 12
Gt. Oaks Chase RG24: Chin . . .6G 9
Gt. Sheldons Coppice
RG27: Hoo 7K 11
Gt. Western Cotts.
RG21: B'toke 3D 16
Grebe Cl. RG22: B'toke 3F 23
Green, The RG25: Over 3D 32
RG28: Whit 6D 30
RG29: N War 4B 20
SP10: Charl 3D 36
SP11: Up C 3D 38
Greenaways, The
RG23: Oak 7B 14
Greenbirch Cl.
RG22: B'toke 3F 23
Greenbury Cl.
RG23: B'toke 4J 15
Greenhaven Cl.
SP10: A'ver 7H 37
Greenlands Rd.
RG24: B'toke 1K 15
Green La. RG27: H Win 3J 13
RG27: Roth 4J 11
Greenly Ct. SP10: A'ver 7E 36
Green Mdws. La.
SP11: G Cla 5F 39
Green Way RG22: B'toke 4J 15
(not continuous)
RG23: B'toke 3J 15
Greenway RG27: Sher L 7G 5
Greenwich Way
SP10: A'ver 4F 37
Greenwood Dr. RG24: Chin . . .4H 9
Greenwoods RG28: Whit 5C 30
Gregory Cl. RG21: B'toke 2E 16
Gregory Ho. RG27: Hoo 7A 12
Gresley Rd. RG21: B'toke 3E 16
Greyhound La.
RG25: Over 4C 32
GREYWELL 6K 19
Greywell Rd.
RG24: Mapl, Old B 4B 18
RG27: A'ell, U Nat 4F 19
Grieg Cl. RG22: B'toke 1A 24
Griffin Way Nth.
RG27: Hoo 5B 12
Griffin Way Sth.
RG27: Hoo 6C 12
Grosvenor Cl.
RG22: B'toke 5H 23
Grosvenor Ho.
RG21: B'toke 4E 16
Grove Cl. RG21: B'toke 6E 16
Grove Ho. RG24: Lych 7H 9
Grove Rd. RG21: B'toke 7D 16
Groves Orchard
RG28: Whit 6B 30
Guernsey Cl. RG24: B'toke 6E 8
Guinea Ct. RG24: Chin 4J 9
Gurney Ct. RG29: Odi 7D 20

H

Hackwood Cl. SP10: A'ver . . .7C 36
Hackwood Cotts.
RG21: B'toke 7E 16
Hackwood La. RG25: Clid . . .4C 24
Hackwood Rd.
RG21: B'toke 5D 16
Hackwood Rd. Roundabout
RG21: B'toke 6E 16
Hadleigh Pl. RG21: B'toke . . .4C 16
Hadrian Rd. SP10: A'ver 3G 37
Hadrians Way
RG23: B'toke 2J 15
Haig Rd. SP10: A'ver 6D 36
Hailstone Rd.
RG21: B'toke 1D 16
Halifax Cl. SP10: A'ver 5E 36
Halliday Cl. RG21: B'toke 7C 16
Halls La. RG27: Matt 1J 11
Hamble Cl. RG23: Oak 1B 22
Hamble Ct. RG21: B'toke 4F 17
Hambledon Way
RG27: Sher L 3K 9
Hamburg Cl. SP10: A'ver 3E 36
Hamelyn Cl. RG21: B'toke 5C 16
Hamelyn Rd. RG21: B'toke 5C 16
Hamilton Cl. RG21: B'toke . . .2A 16
Hammond Rd.
RG21: B'toke 6C 16
HAMPSHIRE BMI CLINIC . . .3G 17
Hampshire Cl.
RG22: Wort 6G 15
Hampshire International Bus. Pk.
RG24: Chin 4G 9
Hampstead Ho.
RG21: B'toke 4D 16
(off Church St.)
Hampton Ct. RG23: B'toke . . .3K 15
Hams Cnr. RG27: Sher L 1C 10
Handel Cl. RG22: B'toke 1A 24
Hanmore Rd. RG24: Chin 6G 9
Hanover Cl. SP10: A'ver 1C 38
Hanover Gdns.
RG21: B'toke 7C 16
Hanover Ho. *SP10: A'ver 7G 37*
(off London St.)
Hanson Rd. SP10: A'ver 5D 36
Hardings La. RG27: H Win . . .2K 13
Hardy La. RG21: B'toke 5C 16
Harebell Cl. RG27: H Win . . .1K 13
Harebell Gdns.
RG27: H Win 1K 13
Hare's La. RG27: H Win 1K 13
Harewood Mobile Home Pk.
SP11: And D 5K 37
Harfield Cl. RG27: Hoo 7A 12
Harlech Cl. RG23: B'toke 4J 15
Harold Jackson Ter.
RG21: B'toke 5E 16
Harris Hill RG22: B'toke 3H 23
Harrison Pl. RG21: B'toke . . .4C 16
Harroway
RG28: Hur P, Whit 3A 30
RG28: Whit 3D 30
Harrow Way SP10: A'ver 5A 36
(not continuous)
Harrow Way, The
RG22: B'toke 1A 24
Hartford Ct. RG27: H Win 2J 13
Hartford Rd. RG27: H Win 2J 13
Hartford Ter. RG27: H Win . . .2K 13
Hart Ho. Ct. RG27: H Win . . .2K 13
Hartley La. RG27: H Wes 5J 5
Hartley Mdw. RG28: Whit 6B 30
Hartley M. *RG27: H Win 1K 13*
(off High St.)
HARTLEY WESPALL 1F 11
HARTLEY WINTNEY 2K 13
Hartswood RG24: Chin 6G 9
Harvest Way RG24: Lych 2H 17
Harveys Fld. RG25: Over 3C 32
Hassocks Workshops
RG24: B'toke 2G 17
Hastings Cl. RG23: B'toke . . .4H 15
HATCH 4B 18
Hatch Cvn. Pk.
RG24: Old B 4A 18
Hatch La. RG24: Old B 3K 17
HATCH WARREN 3H 23
Hatch Warren Cotts.
RG22: B'toke 3J 23
Hatchwarren Gdns.
RG22: B'toke 3A 24
Hatch Warren La.
RG22: B'toke 3H 23
Hatch Warren Retail Pk.
RG22: B'toke 4G 23
Hatch Warren Way
RG22: B'toke 3A 24
Hathaway Gdns.
RG24: B'toke 1F 17
Hatherden Ct. *SP10: A'ver . . .6G 37*
(off Eastfield Rd.)
Hattem Pl. SP10: A'ver 3E 36
Hawk Cl. RG22: B'toke 2F 23
Hawke Cl. SP10: A'ver 5J 37
Hawkes Cl. RG27: H Win 1J 13
Hawkfield La.
RG21: B'toke 5C 16
Hawthorn Ri. RG27: Hoo 6B 12
Hawthorn Way
RG23: B'toke 3J 15
Haydn Rd. RG22: B'toke 2K 23
Hayles Ct. SP10: A'ver 4H 37
Hayley La. RG29: L Sut 5B 28
Haymarket Theatre 5D 16
Haywarden Pl.
RG27: H Win 1K 13
Hazel Cl. RG23: Oak 1B 22
SP10: A'ver 1C 38
Hazelcombe RG25: Over 4D 32
Hazel Coppice RG27: Hoo 6B 12
Hazeldene RG24: Chin 6H 9
Hazeley Cl. RG27: H Win 1J 13
Hazelwood RG24: Chin 4G 9
Hazelwood Cl.
RG23: B'toke 2K 15
Hazelwood Dr.
RG23: B'toke 2K 15
Headington Cl.
RG22: B'toke 2K 23
Heather Dr. SP10: A'ver 5E 36
Heather Gro. RG27: H Win . . .1J 13
Heather La. RG27: U Nat 4G 19
HEATHER ROW 3J 19
Heather Row La.
RG27: Nat S, U Nat 5G 19
Heather Way RG22: B'toke . . .3G 23
Heathfield Rd.
RG22: B'toke 3K 23
Heathside Way
RG27: H Win 1J 13
Heath Va. SP10: A'ver 7G 37
Heathview RG27: Hoo 6C 12
Hedge End Rd.
SP10: A'ver 1G 39
Hedgerows, The
RG24: Lych 1J 17
Hedges Footpath
SP10: A'ver 7E 36
Hele Cl. RG21: B'toke 7C 16
Helford Ct. SP10: A'ver 4H 37
Hendren Sq. SP10: A'ver 4H 37
Hengest Cl. SP10: Charl 3C 36
Hepplewhite Dr.
RG22: B'toke 3G 23
Hepworth Cl. SP10: A'ver 5F 37
Hereford Cl. RG29: Odi 7C 20
Hereford Rd. RG23: B'toke . . .4J 15
Heritage Pk. RG22: B'toke . . .5H 23
Heritage Vw. RG22: B'toke . . .5H 23
Heron Pk. RG24: Lych 7H 9
Herons Ri. SP10: A'ver 1G 39
Heronswood RG29: Odi 5F 21
Heron Way RG22: B'toke 2F 23
Herriard Pl. RG22: B'toke . . .5G 23
Herridge Cl. RG26: B'ley 5E 4
Hesters Vw. RG29: L Sut 7D 28
Hexagon, The SP10: A'ver . . .1C 38
Hibiscus Cres. SP10: A'ver . . .7B 36
Hides Cl. RG28: Whit 7C 30
High Beech Gdns.
SP10: A'ver 7H 37
Highbury Rd. SP11: Ann V . . .3C 38
Highdowns RG22: B'toke 4J 23
High Dr. RG22: B'toke 7J 15
Higher Mead RG24: Lych 1H 17
Highfield Chase
RG21: B'toke 4B 16
Highfields RG25: Over 4D 32
Highland Dr. RG23: Oak 7A 14
Highlands Rd.
RG22: Wort 6G 15
SP10: A'ver 7H 37
Highmoors RG24: Chin 5H 9
Highpath Way
RG24: B'toke 1J 15
High St. RG25: Over 3C 32
RG27: H Win 2K 13
RG29: Odi 6D 20
SP10: A'ver 7F 37
Highwood Ridge
RG22: B'toke 4H 23
Hillary Rd. RG21: B'toke 2B 16
Hillbury Av. SP10: A'ver 1D 38
Hillcrest Ct. RG23: B'toke . . .3H 15
Hillcrest Wlk.
RG23: B'toke 4H 15
Hill Mdw. RG25: Over 1C 32
Hill Rd. RG23: Oak 1A 22
HILL SIDE 7G 21
Hillside RG28: Whit 6E 30
Hillside Ct. SP10: A'ver 7E 36
Hillside Rd. RG29: Odi 1E 28
Hillside Vs. SP10: Charl 4D 36
Hill Sq. RG24: Lych 7J 9
Hillstead Ct.
RG21: B'toke 5D 16
Hilltop Rd. RG25: Over 1D 32
Hill Vw. Rd. RG22: B'toke . . .6A 16
Hobbs Ct. RG24: B'toke 7K 7
Hobbs Sq. *SP10: A'ver 4H 37*
(off Cricketers Way)
HODDINGTON 5G 27
Hogarth Cl. RG21: B'toke 5G 17
Hogarth Ct. SP10: A'ver 4E 36
Holbein Cl. RG21: B'toke 6F 17
Holland Dr. SP10: A'ver 3E 36
Hollies, The RG24: Old B 4B 18
RG27: H Win 4J 13
Hollies Ct. RG24: B'toke 1K 15
Hollies Ind. Est., The
RG24: Old B 4B 18
Hollin's Wlk. *RG21: B'toke . . .4D 16*
(off Festival Pl.)
Holly Cl. RG26: B'ley 5D 4
HOLLY CROSS 2D 4
Holly Dr. RG24: Old B 3A 18

Hollyhock Cl.—Lingen Cl.

Hollyhock Cl. RG22: B'toke . . . 2G 23
Holly Ho. RG24: Old B . . . 4B 18
Holly Wlk. SP10: A'ver . . . 1C 38
Holman Cl. RG26: B'ley . . . 5E 4
Holmes Cl. RG22: B'toke . . . 4J 23
Holmes Ct. SP10: A'ver . . . 7D 36
Holst Cl. RG22: B'toke . . . 3A 24
Holt La. RG27: Hoo . . . 2C 20
Holt Way RG27: Hoo . . . 6C 12
Holy Barn Cl. RG22: B'toke . . . 1G 23
Holyrood Ct. RG22: B'toke . . . 6H 15
Home Farm Gdns. SP10: Charl . . . 3C 36
Homefield Way RG24: B'toke . . . 7J 7
Home Mead RG25: N Wal . . . 2D 34
Homesteads Rd. RG22: B'toke . . . 1G 23
Honeyleaze RG22: B'toke . . . 5G 23
Honeysuckle Cl. RG22: B'toke . . . 2G 23
Honeysuckle Gdns. SP10: A'ver . . . 7B 36
Hood Cl. SP10: A'ver . . . 6J 37
HOOK . . . 7A 12
HOOK COMMON . . . 2K 19
Hook La. RG23: Oak . . . 2A 14
RG26: Up W . . . 2A 14
Hook Rd. RG27: Hoo . . . 2A 20
RG27: Roth . . . 3K 11
RG29: Grey, N War . . . 5K 19
RG29: N War . . . 4C 20
Hook Station (Rail) . . . 1B 20
Hoopersmead RG25: Clid . . . 3C 24
Hoopers Way RG23: Oak . . . 1B 22
Hopfield Rd. RG27: H Win . . . 3J 13
Hop Garden Rd. RG27: Hoo . . . 7K 11
Hopkinson Way SP10: A'ver . . . 5A 36
Hopton Gth. RG24: Lych . . . 7J 9
Hornbeam Pl. RG27: Hoo . . . 6B 12
Horwood Gdns. RG21: B'toke . . . 7B 16
Houghton Sq. RG27: Sher L . . . 3K 9
HOUNDMILLS . . . 3A 16
Houndmills Rd. RG21: B'toke . . . 3A 16
Houndmills Rdbt. RG21: B'toke . . . 2B 16
Hoursome Ct. RG22: B'toke . . . 6H 23
Howard Rd. RG21: B'toke . . . 6E 16
Howard Vw. RG22: B'toke . . . 6K 15
Hubbard Rd. RG21: B'toke . . . 2B 16
Huish La. RG24: Old B . . . 5K 17
RG25: Tun . . . 5K 17
Hulbert Way RG22: B'toke . . . 7J 15
Humberstone Rd. SP10: A'ver . . . 1F 39
Humming Bird Ct. *RG22: B'toke . . . 2F 23* (off Heron Way)
Hundred Acre Rdbt. SP10: A'ver . . . 6B 36
Hungerford La. SP10: K Enh . . . 1F 37
Hunters Cl. RG23: Oak . . . 6B 14
Hunting Ga. SP10: A'ver . . . 6B 36
Hunts Cl. RG27: Hoo . . . 7C 12
Hunts Comn. RG27: H Win . . . 1K 13
Hunts Cotts. RG27: H Win . . . 1K 13
Hurne Ct. *RG21: B'toke . . . 4F 17* (off Lytton Rd.)
Hutton Sq. SP10: A'ver . . . 4H 37
Hyacinth Cl. RG22: B'toke . . . 2G 23
Hyde Rd. RG29: L Sut . . . 7E 28

I

IBWORTH . . . 6A 6
Icknield Ho. SP10: A'ver . . . 4H 37
Icknield Way SP10: A'ver . . . 1G 37
Illingworth Cl. *RG26: B'ley . . . 5E 4* (off St Mary's Av.)
Imperial Ct. SP10: A'ver . . . 5K 37
Inglewood Dr. RG22: B'toke . . . 4H 23
Inkpen Gdns. RG24: Lych . . . 1J 17
Intec Bus. Cen. RG24: B'toke . . . 1G 17
Iris Cl. RG22: B'toke . . . 3G 23
Irwell Cl. RG21: B'toke . . . 4F 17
Isley Rd. RG24: B'toke . . . 6D 8
Itchen Cl. RG23: Oak . . . 1B 22
Itchen Ct. SP10: A'ver . . . 4H 37
Ivar Gdns. RG24: Lych . . . 7J 9

J

Jackdaw Cl. RG22: B'toke . . . 2F 23
Jacob's All. RG21: B'toke . . . 5D 16
Jacob's Yd. RG21: B'toke . . . 5D 16
Jameson Ho. RG24: Lych . . . 7H 9
Jardine Sq. *SP10: A'ver . . . 4H 37* (off Cricketers Way)
Jasmine Ct. *SP10: A'ver . . . 1D 38* (off Floral Way)
Jasmine Rd. RG22: B'toke . . . 2H 23
Jays Cl. RG22: B'toke . . . 1C 24
Jefferson Rd. RG21: B'toke . . . 2D 16
Jellicoe Ct. *SP10: A'ver . . . 5J 37* (off Admirals Way)
Jenson Gdns. SP10: A'ver . . . 7D 36
Jersey Cl. RG24: B'toke . . . 6E 8
Jervis Ct. SP10: A'ver . . . 5J 37
Jibbs Mdw. RG26: B'ley . . . 4C 4
Jobson Cl. RG28: Whit . . . 6C 30
John Eddie Ct. RG22: B'toke . . . 6J 15
John Morgan Cl. RG27: Hoo . . . 6A 12
Joices Yd. RG21: B'toke . . . 5D 16
Joule Rd. RG21: B'toke . . . 2B 16
SP10: A'ver . . . 5A 36
Jubilee Rd. RG21: B'toke . . . 5D 16
Julius Cl. RG24: B'toke . . . 1J 15
Junction Rd. SP10: A'ver . . . 5E 36
June Dr. RG23: B'toke . . . 4H 15
Juniper Cl. RG24: Chin . . . 4J 9
SP10: A'ver . . . 7C 36
Jutland Cres. SP10: A'ver . . . 3E 36

K

Kathleen Cl. RG21: B'toke . . . 7C 16
Keats Cl. RG24: B'toke . . . 7E 8
Kellys Wlk. SP10: A'ver . . . 7D 36
Kelvin Hill RG22: B'toke . . . 6A 16
Kembers La. RG25: Mapl . . . 5C 18
Kemmitt Way SP10: A'ver . . . 1D 38
KEMPSHOTT . . . 1G 23
Kempshott Gdns. RG22: B'toke . . . 2G 23
Kempshott Gro. RG22: Wort . . . 5G 15
Kempshott La. RG22: B'toke . . . 3G 23
Kempshott Pk. Ind. Est. RG23: B'toke . . . 7F 23
Kempshott Rdbt. RG22: B'toke . . . 3H 23
Kemys Gdns. SP10: A'ver . . . 6E 36
Kendal Gdns. RG22: B'toke . . . 7H 15
Kenilworth Rd. RG23: B'toke . . . 3H 15
Kennet Cl. RG21: B'toke . . . 4F 17
Kennet Ct. SP10: A'ver . . . 4H 37
Kennet Way RG23: Oak . . . 1B 22
Kensington Ho. *RG21: B'toke . . . 4D 16* (off Festival Pl.)
Kenyons Yd. SP10: A'ver . . . 6D 36
Kerchers Fld. RG25: Over . . . 4C 32
Kerfield Way RG27: Hoo . . . 7B 12
Kersley Cres. RG29: Odi . . . 2C 28
Kestrel Rd. RG22: B'toke . . . 1F 23
Ketelbey Ri. RG22: B'toke . . . 3B 24
Kew Wlk. SP10: A'ver . . . 7D 36
Keytech Cen. RG23: B'toke . . . 2K 15
Kiel Dr. SP10: A'ver . . . 3E 36
Kiln Gdns. RG27: H Win . . . 2J 13
Kiln La. RG26: M She . . . 3G 7
Kiln Rd. RG24: Sher J . . . 5A 8
Kimbell Rd. RG22: B'toke . . . 7B 16
Kimber Cl. RG24: Chin . . . 6H 9
Kimberley Cl. SP10: Charl . . . 4D 36
Kimberley Rd. RG22: B'toke . . . 6A 16
Kindersley Pk. Homes SP11: Abb A . . . 4A 38
King Arthur's Way SP10: A'ver . . . 3F 37
King Arthur's Way Rdbt. SP10: A'ver . . . 2G 37
Kingfisher Cl. RG22: B'toke . . . 1F 23
RG28: Whit . . . 6C 30
Kingfisher Ct. RG21: B'toke . . . 3C 16
King George Rd. SP10: A'ver . . . 6C 36
King Johns Rd. RG29: N War . . . 5C 20
Kingsbridge Copse RG27: Newn . . . 1J 19
Kingsbridge End *RG27: Hoo . . . 1J 19* (off Old School Rd.)
Kings Chase SP10: A'ver . . . 7D 36
Kingsclere Rd. RG21: B'toke . . . 2B 16
RG23: W Law . . . 4A 6
RG25: Over . . . 1C 32
RG26: Rams, Up W . . . 4A 6
RG28: Whit . . . 3D 30
KING'S FURLONG . . . 6C 16
Kings Furlong Cen. RG21: B'toke . . . 6C 16
King's Furlong Dr. RG21: B'toke . . . 6B 16
Kingsland Bus. Pk. RG24: B'toke . . . 7G 9
Kingsley Pk. RG28: Whit . . . 5C 30
Kingsmead SP11: Ann V . . . 3B 38
Kings Mdw. RG25: Over . . . 3C 32
SP10: A'ver . . . 7G 37
Kingsmill Rd. RG21: B'toke . . . 7C 16
Kings Orchard RG23: Oak . . . 2B 22
Kings Pightle RG24: Chin . . . 5H 9
King's Rd. RG22: B'toke . . . 6A 16
Kingston Cl. SP10: A'ver . . . 1D 38
King St. RG29: Odi . . . 6E 20 (not continuous)
Kingsvale Ct. RG21: B'toke . . . 5B 16 (not continuous)
Kings Wlk. RG28: Whit . . . 6C 30
Kingsway SP10: A'ver . . . 4K 37
Kingsway Gdns. SP10: A'ver . . . 3F 37
Kings Yd. SP10: A'ver . . . 6G 37
Kintyre Cl. RG23: Oak . . . 7A 14
Kipling Wlk. RG22: B'toke . . . 6A 16
Kite Hill Cotts. RG22: Wort . . . 6G 15
Knights Ct. SP10: A'ver . . . 5K 37
KNIGHTS ENHAM . . . 1F 37
Knights Enham Rdbt. SP10: A'ver . . . 2F 37
Knights Pk. Rd. RG21: B'toke . . . 3B 16
Knight St. RG21: B'toke . . . 5B 16
Knowle Rd. RG24: B'toke . . . 1J 15
Knowle Vw. RG28: Whit . . . 7D 30
Knowlings, The RG28: Whit . . . 7D 30

L

Laburnum Way RG23: B'toke . . . 3K 15
Ladies Wlk. SP10: A'ver . . . 1H 39
Laffans Rd. RG29: Odi . . . 1D 28
Laker Sq. SP10: A'ver . . . 4H 37
Lakeside Cl. SP10: Charl . . . 4C 36
Lake Vw. RG27: H Win . . . 1K 13
Lamb Cl. SP10: A'ver . . . 7H 37
Lamb Rdbt., The SP10: A'ver . . . 7G 37
Lambs Cl. RG25: Over . . . 3D 32
Lambs Row RG24: Lych . . . 2H 17
Lampards Cl. RG27: Roth . . . 2K 11
Lancaster Cl. SP10: A'ver . . . 5E 36
Lancaster Rd. RG21: B'toke . . . 3C 16
Landseer Cl. RG21: B'toke . . . 6F 17
Landseer Ct. SP10: A'ver . . . 5E 36
LANE END . . . 7G 29
Lane End RG26: B'ley . . . 5C 4
Lane's End RG24: Chin . . . 6J 9
Lansdowne Av. SP10: A'ver . . . 1D 38
Lansley Rd. RG21: B'toke . . . 1D 16
Lapin La. RG22: B'toke . . . 5H 23
Lapwing Cl. RG22: B'toke . . . 3F 23
Lapwing Ri. RG28: Whit . . . 6B 30
Larch Dr. SP10: A'ver . . . 7B 36
Larchwood RG24: Chin . . . 5H 9
Lark Cl. RG22: B'toke . . . 2F 23
SP10: A'ver . . . 4G 37
Larkfield RG24: Chin . . . 6H 9
Larks Barrow Hill RG28: Whit . . . 1C 30
Larkspur Gdns. RG21: B'toke . . . 6B 16
Larwood Sq. *SP10: A'ver . . . 4H 37* (off Cricketers Way)
Launcelot Cl. SP10: A'ver . . . 3F 37
Laundry Yd. RG28: Whit . . . 6C 30
Laurel Cl. RG23: Oak . . . 1B 22
RG29: N War . . . 6C 20
Laurels, The RG21: B'toke . . . 3E 16
SP10: A'ver . . . 5D 36
Lauriston Ct. RG21: B'toke . . . 5E 16
Lavender Ct. *SP10: A'ver . . . 1D 38* (off Floral Way)
Lavender Rd. RG22: B'toke . . . 3G 23
LAVERSTOKE . . . 6J 31
Laverstoke La. RG28: Lave . . . 7H 31
Lavington Cotts. RG24: Old B . . . 1K 17
Lawrence Cl. RG24: B'toke . . . 7E 8
SP10: A'ver . . . 4E 36
Lawrencedale Ct. RG21: B'toke . . . 5B 16
Lay Fld. RG27: Hoo . . . 7K 11
Lea Cl. RG21: B'toke . . . 4F 17
Leaden Vere RG29: L Sut . . . 6D 28
Lees Hill RG29: S War . . . 6J 27
Lees Mdw. RG27: Hoo . . . 7C 12
Lee Vw. SP11: Up C . . . 3D 38
Lefroy Av. RG21: B'toke . . . 2E 16
Lehar Cl. RG22: B'toke . . . 2K 23
Leicester Pl. SP10: A'ver . . . 7F 37
Leigh Cl. SP10: A'ver . . . 7H 37
Leigh Gdns. SP10: A'ver . . . 7H 37
Leigh Rd. SP10: A'ver . . . 7G 37
Lennon Way RG22: B'toke . . . 2J 23
Lennox Mall RG22: B'toke . . . 7A 16
Lennox Rd. RG22: B'toke . . . 7A 16
Len Smart Ct. RG21: B'toke . . . 1E 16
Lewis Cl. RG21: B'toke . . . 2E 16
Leyton Way SP10: A'ver . . . 1C 38
Lightfoot Gro. RG21: B'toke . . . 7D 16
Lightsfield RG23: Oak . . . 7B 14
Lilac Cl. SP10: A'ver . . . 7C 36
Lilac Way RG23: B'toke . . . 3K 15
Lillymill Chine RG24: Old B . . . 6J 9
Lillywhite Cres. SP10: A'ver . . . 2G 37
Lily Cl. RG22: B'toke . . . 2G 23
Limbrey Hill RG25: Up G . . . 5G 27
Lime Gdns. RG21: B'toke . . . 4F 17
Limes, The RG22: B'toke . . . 2G 23
RG26: B'ley . . . 5E 4
Lime Tree Way RG24: Chin . . . 5G 9
Lime Wlk. SP10: A'ver . . . 1C 38
Lincoln Cl. RG22: B'toke . . . 3H 23
Linden Av. RG24: Old B . . . 4K 17
RG29: Odi . . . 5F 21
Linden Ct. RG24: Old B . . . 4K 17
Lindenwood RG24: Chin . . . 4F 9
Lingen Cl. SP10: A'ver . . . 3E 36

46 A-Z Basingstoke

Lingfield Cl. RG24: Old B 4A 18
Link, The SP10: A'ver 6B 36
Link Way RG23: Oak 1B 22
Linnet Cl. RG22: B'toke ...7G 15
Linton Dr. SP10: A'ver 5E 36
Lion Cl. RG25: Over 4C 32
Lion Ct. RG24: B'toke 2H 17
Lisa Ct. RG21: B'toke 5C 16
Lister Rd. RG22: B'toke ...7B 16
Litchfield Cl. SP10: Charl ...3C 36
Little Basing RG24: Old B ...2H 17
Lit. Binfields RG24: Old B ...7J 9
Little Copse SP10: A'ver ...1D 38
Lit. Copse Chase
  RG24: Chin 6G 9
Lit. Dean La. RG25: Up G ...6H 27
Little Fallow RG24: Lych 1H 17
Lit. Hartleys RG27: Hoo ...7D 12
Lit. Hoddington
  RG25: Up G 5G 27
Lit. Hoddington Cl.
  RG25: Up G 5G 27
Litton Gdns. RG23: Oak ...1B 22
Livia Cl. SP10: A'ver 2G 37
Livingstone Rd.
  SP10: A'ver 5K 37
Locksbridge La.
  RG26: B'ley 5A 4
Locksmead RG21: B'toke ...4F 17
Lock Sq. SP10: A'ver 4H 37
Loddon Bus. Cen.
  RG24: B'toke 2G 17
Loddon Cen., The
  RG24: B'toke 1G 17
Loddon Ct. RG21: B'toke ...7D 16
Loddon Dr. RG21: B'toke ...4E 16
Loddon Ho. RG21: B'toke ...3E 16
Loddon Mall RG21: B'toke ..4D 16
Loddon Vale Indoor Bowling
  Club, The 4K 15
Lodge Cl. SP10: A'ver 6D 36
Loggon Rd. RG21: B'toke ...7C 16
Lomond Cl. RG23: Oak 7A 14
London Rd. RG21: B'toke ...5E 16
  RG24: Old B 5G 17
  RG25: Over 3D 32
  RG27: H Win 1K 13
  RG27: H Win, Hoo 6C 12
  RG27: Nat S, Old B ...3D 18
  RG28: Whit 6D 30
  RG29: Odi 6E 20
    (not continuous)
  SP10: A'ver 7G 37
  SP11: A'ver, And D ...6K 37
London St. RG21: B'toke ...5D 16
  RG28: Whit 6C 30
  SP10: A'ver 7G 37
Longacre Ri. RG24: Chin ...6G 9
Longbridge Cl.
  RG27: Sher L 6H 5
Longbridge Rd. RG26: B'ley ...4C 4
Long Copse Chase
  RG24: Chin 6G 9
Longcroft Cl. RG21: B'toke ...5C 16
Long Cross La.
  RG22: B'toke 4G 23
Longfellow Pde.
  RG22: B'toke 1E 16
Longfield RG23: Oak 6B 14
Longfield Cl. RG25: N Wal ...2C 34
Long La. RG24: Old B 6J 9
    (not continuous)
  RG29: Odi, Wel 1E 28
Longmoor Rd.
  RG21: B'toke 5C 16
Longparish Ct.
  SP10: A'ver 7G 37
    (off London Rd.)
Longroden La. RG25: Tun ...4K 25
Longs Ct. RG28: Whit 6C 30
    (not continuous)
Longstock Cl. RG24: Chin ...4K 9
  SP10: A'ver 7D 36
Longstock Ct. SP10: A'ver ...7G 37
    (off London Rd.)
Longsutton Rd. SP11: G Cla ...7F 39
LONG SUTTON 7D 28
Longwood Copse La.
  RG22: B'toke 6F 23
  RG23: B'toke 6F 23

Lordsfield Gdns.
  RG25: Over 3C 32
Lovegroves RG24: Chin 5J 9
Love La. RG29: Odi 2D 28
    (not continuous)
  SP10: A'ver 7G 37
Loveridge Cl.
  RG21: B'toke 7C 16
  SP10: A'ver 2G 37
Lwr. Brook St.
  RG21: B'toke 4B 16
Lwr. Chestnut Dr.
  RG21: B'toke 6B 16
Lwr. Evingar Rd.
  RG28: Whit 6C 30
Lowlands Rd.
  RG22: B'toke 6G 15
Lowry Ct. SP10: A'ver 5E 36
Loyalty La. RG24: Old B ...3K 17
Lubeck Dr. SP10: A'ver ...3E 36
Ludlow Cl. RG23: B'toke ...4J 15
Ludlow Gdns.
  RG23: B'toke 4K 15
Lundy Cl. RG24: B'toke ...7F 9
Lune Cl. RG21: B'toke 4F 17
Lune Ct. SP10: A'ver 4H 37
Lupin Cl. RG22: B'toke ...2G 23
Lutyens Cl. RG24: Lych ...7H 9
LYCHPIT 1H 17
Lyde Cl. RG23: Oak 1B 22
LYDE GREEN 1H 11
Lyford Rd. RG21: B'toke ...3D 16
Lymington Cl.
  RG22: B'toke 3H 23
LYNCH 3A 32
Lynch, The RG25: Over 3A 32
  RG28: Whit 6D 30
LYNCH HILL 6D 30
Lynch Hill RG24: Whit 6C 30
Lynch Hill Pk. RG28: Whit ...5D 30
Lyn Ct. RG21: B'toke 4F 17
Lyndhurst Dr. RG22: B'toke ...4J 23
Lynwood Dr. SP10: A'ver ...6D 36
Lynwood Gdns.
  RG27: Hoo 7A 12
Lyttel Combe RG27: Hoo ...7D 12
Lytton Rd. RG21: B'toke ...4E 16

M

Mabbs La. RG27: H Win ...4J 13
Mabelmyll Cft. RG27: Hoo ...7D 12
Macadam Way
  SP10: A'ver 5A 36
McCartney Wlk.
  RG22: B'toke 3J 23
McFauld Way RG28: Whit ...7D 30
Madeira Cl. RG24: B'toke ...7F 9
Madrid Rd. SP10: A'ver ...5H 37
Magellan Cl. SP10: A'ver ...5K 37
Magnolia Cl. SP10: A'ver ...7D 36
Magnolia Ct. RG24: Sher J ...7C 8
Magnus Dr. RG22: B'toke ...3H 23
Magpie Cl. RG22: B'toke ...2F 23
Mahler Cl. RG22: B'toke ...2B 24
Maidenthorn La.
  RG25: N Wal 2D 34
Majestic Rd. RG22: B'toke ...4G 23
Majorca Av. SP10: A'ver ...5H 37
Maldive Rd. RG24: B'toke ...7F 9
Malham Gdns.
  RG22: B'toke 5H 23
Mall, The SP10: A'ver 7F 37
    (off Bridge St.)
Mallard Cl. RG22: B'toke ...3F 23
  SP10: A'ver 4G 37
Malls Shop. Cen., The
  RG21: B'toke 4D 16
Malmesbury Flds.
  RG22: B'toke 2K 23
Malshanger La.
  RG23: Oak 5A 14
Malta Cl. RG21: B'toke 7D 8
Maltings, The RG26: B'ley ...5C 4
Malvern Cl. RG22: B'toke ...6G 15
Manley James Cl.
  RG29: Odi 6E 20
Mann Cl. RG28: Whit 7D 30
Manor Cl. RG22: B'toke ...4G 23

Manor Copse SP10: K Enh ...1G 37
Manor Cotts. RG28: Free ...5H 31
Manor Ho. RG22: Lych 1H 17
Manor La. RG24: Old B ...3K 17
Manor Ri. SP11: Ann V 3D 38
Manor Rise Flats
  SP11: Ann V 3D 38
Manor Rd. RG22: Sher J ...5A 8
  SP10: A'ver 5E 36
Mansell Ct. RG28: Whit ...5C 30
Mansfield Rd.
  RG22: B'toke 7A 16
Manydown Pk.
  RG23: W Law 4C 14
Maple Cl. RG22: Wort 5H 15
Maple Cres. RG21: B'toke ...2D 16
MAPLEDURWELL 5D 18
Maplehurst Chase
  RG22: B'toke 4H 23
Mapletons, The RG29: Odi ...6F 21
Maple Wlk. SP10: A'ver ...1C 38
Maplewood RG24: Chin 5G 9
Marchant Rd. SP10: A'ver ...7D 36
March Cl. SP10: A'ver 5G 37
Margaret Rd.
  RG22: B'toke 5K 15
Marguerite Cl. RG26: B'ley ...4C 4
Marigold Cl. RG22: B'toke ...2G 23
Market Chambers
  RG21: B'toke 5D 16
    (off Church St.)
Market Pl. RG21: B'toke ...5D 16
  RG28: Whit 6C 30
Mark La. RG21: B'toke 5D 16
  SP10: A'ver 4A 36
  SP11: Pen C 5A 36
Marlborough Gdns.
  RG23: Oak 7B 14
Marlborough St.
  SP10: A'ver 6F 37
Marlborough Trad. M.
  RG24: Chin 6F 9
Marlowe Cl. RG24: B'toke ...1E 16
Marl's La.
  RG24: B'toke, Sher J ...3D 8
Marsden Ct. RG28: Lave ...5J 31
Marshall Gdns.
  RG21: B'toke 2D 16
Marshall Sq. SP10: A'ver ...4H 37
    (off Cricketers Way)
Marshcourt RG24: Lych 1H 17
Marsum Cl. SP10: A'ver ...2E 36
Martin Cl. RG21: B'toke ...2E 16
Martins Wood RG24: Chin ...5H 9
Martin Way SP10: A'ver ...4G 37
Mary La. RG25: N Wal 1C 34
Mary Rose Ct.
  RG21: B'toke 5B 16
Maslen M. RG22: B'toke ...6H 23
Mathias Wlk.
  RG22: B'toke 4K 23
Matilda Dr. RG22: B'toke ...3H 23
Matthews Way RG23: Oak ...1C 22
Mattock Way RG24: Chin ...5G 9
Maw Cl. RG22: B'toke 2B 24
Maybrook RG24: Chin 4H 9
May Cl. RG24: Old B 3A 18
Mayfair Ho. RG21: B'toke ...4D 16
    (off Festival Pl.)
Mayfield Ridge
  RG22: B'toke 5H 23
Mayflower Cl. RG24: Chin ...6G 9
Maynard's Wood
  RG24: Chin 6G 9
May Pl. RG21: B'toke 5D 16
May St. RG21: B'toke 4B 16
May Tree Rd. SP10: A'ver ...5C 36
Mead, The RG24: Old B ...3K 17
Mead Cl. SP10: A'ver 7E 36
Mead Gdns. RG27: H Win ...1H 13
Mead Hatchgate
  RG27: Hoo 6A 12
Mead Hedges SP10: A'ver ...1D 38
Mead Hedges Footpath
  SP10: A'ver 1E 38
Meadow Cvn. Site
  RG27: James L 6G 5
Meadow Dr. SP11: G Cla ...7F 39
Meadowland RG24: Chin ...5G 9
Meadow La. RG27: H Win ...2J 13

Meadowridge
  RG22: B'toke 4J 23
Meadow Ri. RG25: N Wal ...2D 34
Meadow Rd. RG21: B'toke ...7C 16
Meadows, The
  RG27: Sher L 6G 5
Meadow Vw. RG28: Whit ...6B 30
Meadow Way SP10: A'ver ...6C 36
Mead Rd. SP10: A'ver 7E 36
Mead Vw. SP11: G Cla 6F 39
Mede Cl. RG25: Over 4D 32
Medina Gdns. RG23: Oak ...1B 22
Medway Av. RG23: Oak ...7B 14
Medway Ct. RG21: B'toke ...4F 17
  SP10: A'ver 4H 37
Meitner Cl. RG26: B'ley ...3C 4
Melford Gdns.
  RG22: Wort 7G 15
Meliot Ri. SP10: A'ver 2F 37
Melrose Wlk.
  RG22: B'toke 1B 16
Memorial Bungalows
  RG28: Lave 6H 31
Memorial Rd. RG27: Hoo ...1A 20
Mendip Cl. RG22: B'toke ...6G 15
Meon Rd. RG23: Oak 1B 22
Meon Wlk. RG21: B'toke ...4E 16
Mercer Cl. RG22: B'toke ...5J 15
Mercia Av. SP10: Charl ...3C 36
Meridian Office Pk.
  RG27: Hoo 1B 20
Merlin Mead RG22: B'toke ...4F 23
Merriatt Cl. RG21: B'toke ...7D 16
Merrileas Gdns.
  RG22: B'toke 2G 23
Merrydown La. RG24: Chin ...6J 9
Merryfield RG24: Chin 5G 9
Mersey Ct. SP10: A'ver ...4H 37
Merton Rd. RG21: B'toke ...3B 16
Mews, The RG26: B'ley ...5E 4
  RG28: Whit 7D 30
Micheldever Gdns.
  RG28: Whit 7D 30
Micheldever Rd.
  RG28: Whit 7C 30
  SP10: A'ver 7G 37
  SP11: A'ver 7G 37
Middle Mead RG27: Hoo ...7A 12
Middleton Gdns.
  RG22: B'toke 2D 16
Midlane Cl. RG21: B'toke ...7C 16
Mildmay Cl. RG21: B'toke ...7E 20
Mildmay Ter. RG27: H Win ...2K 13
Milestones, Hampshire Living
  History Mus. 4A 16
Milkingpen La.
  RG24: Old B 3K 17
Millard Cl. RG21: B'toke ...2B 16
Mill Cl. RG27: Sher L 6H 5
Millennium Ct.
  RG21: B'toke 4B 16
Mill La. RG7: Stra S 1E 4
  RG27: H Wes 7K 5
  RG27: Sher L 1E 4
  RG29: N War 5B 20
Mill Rd. RG24: B'toke 1J 15
Millstream Cl. SP10: A'ver ...1E 38
Mill Vw. RG29: Grey 7K 19
Millway Cl. SP10: A'ver ...7D 36
Millway Rd. SP10: A'ver ...7D 36
Milton Av. SP10: A'ver ...5C 36
Milton Ct. RG24: B'toke ...1E 16
Mimosa Cl. SP10: A'ver ...1D 38
Minchens La. RG26: B'ley ...4B 4
Minden Cl. RG24: Chin ...6G 9
  SP10: A'ver 3E 36
Minshull Cl. SP10: A'ver ...6E 36
Mitchell Av. RG27: H Win ...3J 13
Mitchell Cl. SP10: A'ver ...5A 36
Mitchell Gdns.
  RG22: B'toke 3J 23
Moat Cl. RG26: B'ley 3C 4
Monachus La.
  RG27: H Win 1K 13
Monarch Cl. RG22: B'toke ...4G 23
Moneyer Rd. SP10: A'ver ...3E 36
Mongers Piece RG24: Chin ...4J 9
Moniton Est. RG22: Wort ...5H 15
MONK SHERBORNE 2H 7
Monk Sherborne Ho.
  RG26: M She 3H 7

Monk Sherborne Rd.
RG24: Sher J 3H 7
RG26: Cha A, Rams 1D 6
RG26: M She 2H 7
Montague Pl.
RG21: B'toke 6D 16
Montserrat Pl. RG24: B'toke . . .6E 8
Montserrat Rd.
RG24: B'toke 6E 8
Monxton Rd. SP10: A'ver 6A 36
SP11: A'ver 7A 36
Monxton Rd. Rdbt.
SP11: A'ver 6A 36
Moore Cl. SP10: A'ver 5F 37
Moorfoot Gdns.
RG22: B'toke 6H 15
Moorhams Av.
RG22: B'toke 4G 23
Moorings, The
RG21: B'toke 4F 17
Moor Vw. RG24: Old B 2K 17
Moot Cl. SP10: A'ver 2G 37
Morgaston Rd.
RG26: B'ley, M She 2K 7
Morley Rd. RG21: B'toke 1C 24
Mornington Cl.
SP10: A'ver 2F 39
Morris Ri. RG24: Chin 6G 9
Morris St. RG27: Hoo 1J 19
Morse Rd. RG22: B'toke 5A 16
Mortimer Cl.
RG27: H Win 4H 13
Mortimer La. RG7: Stra S 1E 4
RG21: B'toke 4C 16
Moscrop Ct. RG21: B'toke . .5C 16
Moulshay La.
RG27: Sher L 3A 10
Mountbatten Ct.
SP10: A'ver 5J 37
Mountbatten Ho.
RG21: B'toke 3F 17
RG28: Free 5H 31
Mourne Cl. RG22: B'toke . . .5H 15
Mozart Cl. RG22: B'toke . . .2A 24
Mulberry Mead
RG28: Whit 6C 30
Mulberry Way RG24: Chin . . .5H 9
Mull Cl. RG23: Oak 7A 14
Mullins Cl. RG21: B'toke . . .1D 16
Munnings Cl. RG21: B'toke . .6F 17
Munnings Cl. SP10: A'ver . . .5E 36
Murray Cl. SP10: A'ver 2E 38
Murrell Grn. Bus. Pk.
RG27: Hoo 6E 12
Murrell Grn. Rd.
RG27: H Win 3E 12
Musgrave Cl.
RG22: B'toke 2K 23
Musket Copse RG24: Old B . .3J 17
Mylen Bus. Cen.
SP10: A'ver 6D 36
Mylen Rd. SP10: A'ver 6D 36
Myllers Lond RG27: Hoo 7D 12

Napier Wlk. SP10: A'ver 5J 37
Napoleon Dr. RG23: B'toke . . .2J 15
Nash Cl. RG21: B'toke 2E 16
Nash Mdws. RG29: S War . . .6K 27
Nately Rd. RG27: U Nat 6H 19
RG29: Grey 6H 19
Neath Rd. RG21: B'toke 4C 4
Nelson Wlk. SP10: A'ver 5J 37
Nene Ct. SP10: A'ver 4H 37
Nestor Cl. SP10: A'ver 5E 36
Neuvic Way RG28: Whit 7D 30
Neville Cl. RG21: B'toke 1G 16
SP10: A'ver 1G 39
Neville Cl. RG24: B'toke 2G 17
New Bri. La. RG21: B'toke . . .4F 17
Newbury La.
SP11: Charl, Pen M 2A 36
Newbury Rd. RG28: Whit 6C 30
SP10: A'ver, K Enh 2F 37
SP11: Enh A 2F 37

Newbury Rd. Junc.
RG24: B'toke 2K 15
Newbury St. RG28: Whit 6C 30
SP10: A'ver 6G 37
Newcomb Cl. SP10: A'ver . . .2E 38
Newman Bassett Ho.
RG23: B'toke 3J 15
New Mkt. Sq.
RG21: B'toke 4D 16
Newnham La.
RG24: Old B 1K 17
RG27: Newn 1K 17
Newnham Pk. RG27: Hoo . . .1K 19
Newnham Rd.
RG27: Newn 1H 19
New North Dr.
RG27: Sher L 1C 10
New Rd. RG21: B'toke 4D 16
RG26: B'ley 1C 8
RG27: H Win 2J 13
RG27: Hoo 1A 20
RG29: N War 5C 20
New St. RG21: B'toke 5D 16
SP10: A'ver 4G 37
Newton Pk. SP10: A'ver 5A 36
Newtown Cl. SP10: A'ver 7D 36
Nightingale Gdns.
RG24: B'toke 1J 15
RG27: Hoo 7A 12
Nightingale Ri.
RG25: Over 4D 32
Nobs Crook RG27: Hoo 7C 12
Norden Cl. RG21: B'toke . . .3D 16
Norden Ho. RG21: B'toke . . .3E 16
Norman Ct. La.
SP11: Up C 2E 38
Normanton Rd.
RG21: B'toke 2D 16
Norn Hill RG21: B'toke 3E 16
Norn Hill Cl. RG21: B'toke . .3E 16
Norrie Ct. RG24: B'toke 1J 15
Northbrook Cres.
RG24: B'toke 1J 15
Northcroft Ct.
RG29: S War 7A 28
Northern Av. SP10: A'ver . . .5F 37
Northern Retail Pk.
SP10: A'ver 5F 37
North Fld. RG25: Over 2C 32
Northfield Rd.
RG27: Sher L 6G 5
Northgate Way
RG22: B'toke 4G 23
North Row RG26: B'ley 3C 4
Nth. Waltham Rd.
RG23: Oak . . . . .3A 22 & 4A 22
North Way SP10: A'ver 4J 37
Norton Ho. RG22: B'toke . . .6J 15
Norton Ride RG24: Lych 2H 17
Norwich Cl. RG22: B'toke . . .3H 23
Novello Cl. RG22: B'toke . . .3K 23
Nursery Cl. RG24: Chin 5J 9
RG27: Hoo 6A 12
Nursery Ter. RG29: N War . . .5C 20
Nutbane Cl. SP10: A'ver 7C 36
Nuthatch Cl. RG22: B'toke . .4F 23
Nutley La. RG25: Dumm 2K 35

Oak Bank SP10: A'ver 1F 39
Oak Cl. RG21: B'toke 4F 17
RG23: Oak 1B 22
RG25: Over 4C 32
Oakfields RG24: Lych 1H 17
Oak Hanger Cl.
RG27: Hoo 7B 12
Oakland Rd. RG28: Whit 6C 30
Oaklands RG27: H Win 3J 13
Oaklands Pk. RG27: Hoo . . .2J 19
Oaklands Way
RG23: B'toke 3J 15
Oakland Ter. RG27: H Win . . .2K 13

Oaklea Gdns. RG26: B'ley 5E 4
Oakley La. RG23: Oak 1A 22
Oakley Pl. RG27: H Win 2K 13
(off High St.)
Oakmead RG26: B'ley 3B 4
Oakridge Ho. RG21: B'toke . .2E 16
Oakridge Rd.
RG21: B'toke 2B 16
Oakridge Towers
RG21: B'toke 2E 16
Oak Tree Dr. RG27: Hoo 6B 12
Oakwood RG24: Chin 5G 9
(Crockford La.)
RG24: Chin 5H 9
(Hanmore Rd.)
Oakwood Ct. RG27: H Win . . .2J 13
Oasts, The RG29: L Sut 6D 28
Oban Cl. RG23: Oak 7A 14
Oceana Cres.
RG22: B'toke 6F 23
Ochil Cl. RG22: B'toke 6H 15
Octavian Cl. RG22: B'toke . .3H 23
Odeon Cinema
West Ham 4K 15
Odiham Castle (Remains of)
. . . . .5A 20
Odiham Rd. RG27: Win 4H 13
RG29: Odi, Win 3F 21
Officers Row RG26: B'ley 5E 4
Olaf Cl. SP10: A'ver 2G 37
Old Barn Cl. RG25: N Wal . . .2C 34
Old Basing Mall
RG21: B'toke 4D 16
Oldberg Gdns.
RG22: B'toke 2B 24
Old Brick Kiln Trad. Est., The
RG26: Rams 1E 6
Old Canal Pl. RG21: B'toke . .4F 17
Old Chapel La.
RG26: Cha A 1F 7
Old Comn. Rd.
RG21: B'toke 5F 17
Old Down Cl.
RG22: B'toke 2G 23
Old Down Rd. SP10: A'ver . . .5E 36
Oldenburg Cl. SP10: A'ver . . .5E 36
Old English Dr.
SP10: A'ver 2E 36
Oldfield Vw. RG27: H Win . . .3J 13
Old Kempshott La.
RG22: Wort 7G 15
Old Orchard, The
RG29: S War 6K 27
Old Potbridge Rd.
RG27: Win 7G 13
Old Reading Rd.
RG21: B'toke 3E 16
Old Rectory, The
RG29: S War 7A 28
Old Salisbury Rd.
SP11: Abb A 4A 38
Old School Cl.
RG27: H Win 2K 13
Old School Rd. RG27: Hoo . . .1J 19
Old Winton Rd.
SP10: A'ver 7G 37
Old Worting Rd.
RG22: B'toke, Wort 5J 15
Olivers Cl. RG26: B'ley 5D 4
Oliver's La. RG26: B'ley 3D 4
Oliver's Wlk. RG24: Lych 2H 17
Onslow Cl. RG24: B'toke 7G 9
Orchard, The RG25: Over . . .4C 32
RG27: Hoo 6A 12
Orchard Lea RG27: Sher L . . .7G 5
Orchard Pl. RG28: Whit 6C 30
(off Church St.)
Orchard Rd. RG22: B'toke . . .4H 23
SP10: A'ver 5D 36
Orchid Ct. SP10: A'ver 1C 38
(off Floral Way)
Orkney Cl. RG24: B'toke 7F 9
Osborne Cl. RG21: B'toke . . .2C 16
Osborne Rd. SP10: A'ver . . .7E 36

Osborn Ind. Est.
RG27: Hoo 1B 20
Osborn Way RG27: Hoo 1B 20
Osler Cl. RG26: B'ley 4C 4
Osprey Rd. RG22: B'toke . . .1F 23
Otterbourne Wlk.
RG27: Sher L 3K 9
Oval, The SP10: A'ver 3H 37
Ox Drove
SP11: And D, Pic P 6K 37
Oyster Cl. RG22: B'toke 3H 23

Packenham Rd.
RG21: B'toke 6B 16
Pack La. RG22: B'toke 7G 15
RG23: Oak, Wort 6B 14
Paddington Ho.
RG21: B'toke 4D 16
(off Festival Pl.)
Paddock, The
RG27: H Win 1K 13
Paddock Ct. RG27: H Win . . .3J 13
Paddockfields
RG24: Old B 2K 17
Paddock Rd. RG22: B'toke . .6K 15
Paddock Wlk.
RG21: B'toke 6K 15
Padwick Cl. RG21: B'toke . .5C 16
Pages Bungalows
RG27: Hoo 4E 16
Painters Pightle
RG27: Hoo 7K 11
Palace Ga. RG29: Odi 6D 20
Palace Ga. Farm
RG29: Odi 6D 20
Palmer Dr. SP10: A'ver 6J 37
Palmerston Pl.
SP10: A'ver 6J 37
Pantile Dr. RG27: Hoo 7C 12
Papermakers RG25: Over . . .4D 32
Parade, The RG21: B'toke . . .3E 16
Pardown RG23: Oak 3B 22
Park & Ride
Leisure Park 4K 15
Park Av. RG24: Old B 4K 9
Park Cl. RG23: Oak 7A 14
Park Cnr. Rd.
RG27: H Win 1K 13
Park Gdns. RG21: B'toke . . .6E 16
Park Hill RG24: Old B 3J 17
Park La. RG24: Old B 4K 17
Pk. Prewett Rd.
RG24: B'toke 1J 15
Parkside Rd. RG21: B'toke . .6E 16
Parkview Cl. SP10: A'ver 4D 36
Parkwood Cl. RG24: Chin . . .4H 9
Parnell Ct. SP10: A'ver 5B 36
Partridge Cl.
RG22: B'toke 3F 23
Paterson Cl. RG22: B'toke . .3J 23
Paulet Pl. RG24: Old B 3K 17
Paxton Cl. RG22: B'toke . . .3H 23
Paynes Mdw. RG24: Lych . . .1J 17
Peake Cl. RG24: Lych 2H 17
Pearman Dr. SP10: A'ver . . .6J 37
Pear Tree Way
RG21: B'toke 2E 16
Pecche Pl. RG24: Old B 6J 9
Peel Ct. RG27: H Win 2J 13
Pegasus Cl. RG28: Whit 5C 30
Peked Mede RG27: Hoo 7D 12
Pekelond RG27: Hoo 7D 12
Pelham Cl. RG24: Old B 4K 17
Pelican Ct. SP10: A'ver 5G 37
Pelton Rd. RG21: B'toke . . .3B 16
Pembroke Ct. SP10: A'ver . . .6G 37
Pembroke Rd.
RG23: B'toke 4H 15
Pemerton Rd.
RG21: B'toke 2E 16
Pen Cl. SP10: A'ver 7H 37
Pendennis Cl.
RG23: B'toke 3H 15

Pendennis Ct.
RG23: B'toke 3H 15
Pennine Cl. RG22: B'toke . . .6H 15
Pennine Way
RG22: B'toke 6H 15
Penrith Rd. RG21: B'toke . . .5C 16
Pensdell Farm Cotts.
RG25: Clid 1D 24
Pentland Cl. RG22: B'toke . . .6H 15
Penton Way
RG24: B'toke, Sher J . . .6D 8
Pershore Rd. RG24: B'toke . .7D 8
(not continuous)
Pesthouse La. RG28: Whit . .5C 30
Petersfield RG23: Oak 2B 22
Petersfield Cl. RG24: Chin . .4K 9
Petrel Cft. RG22: B'toke 2F 23
Petty's Brook Rd.
RG24: Chin 4J 9
Petunia Cl. RG22: B'toke . . .2G 23
Petworth Cl. RG22: B'toke . .4H 23
Peveral Wlk. RG22: B'toke . .5K 15
Peveral Way RG22: B'toke . .6K 15
Pexalls Cl. RG27: Hoo 7C 12
Pheaben's Fld.
RG26: B'ley 4B 4
Pheasant Cl. RG22: B'toke . .2F 23
Pheby Rd. RG22: B'toke . . .7K 15
Phoenix Ct. RG27: H Win . .4H 13
PHOENIX GREEN **4H 13**
Phoenix Grn.
RG27: H Win 4H 13
Phoenix Pk. Ter.
RG21: B'toke 3D 16
Phoenix Ter. RG27: H Win . .4H 13
Picket Twenty SP11: A'ver . .6K 37
Picton Rd. SP10: A'ver 2E 38
Pigeon Cl. RG26: B'ley 5D 4
Pigeonhouse La.
RG25: Far W 7A 24
Pilgrims Way SP10: A'ver . .4H 37
Pimpernel Way
RG24: Lych 2H 17
Pines, The SP10: A'ver 6E 36
Pine Wlk. SP10: A'ver 1C 38
Pinewood RG24: Chin 5F 9
Pinkerton Rd.
RG22: B'toke 7J 15
Pinnell Cl. RG22: B'toke . . .4G 23
Pintail Cl. RG22: B'toke 3F 23
Pitcairn Cl. RG24: B'toke . . .6E 8
Pither Rd. RG29: Odi 2C 28
Pitman Cl. RG22: B'toke . . .7H 15
Pittard Rd. RG21: B'toke . . .6B 16
Pitts La. SP10: A'ver 1F 39
Planet Ice **4J 15**
Plantation, The
RG27: Sher L 7J 9
Plantation Rd. SP10: A'ver . .7D 36
Plover Cl. RG22: B'toke 1G 23
SP10: A'ver 4G 37
Poachers Fld.
RG29: S War 7A 28
Poland La. RG29: Odi 3E 20
POLECAT CORNER **1K 25**
POLHAMPTON **1F 33**
Pond Cl. RG25: Over 5C 32
Pond Cotts. RG25: Clid 3C 24
Pond Rd. RG26: B'ley 5D 4
Pool Rd. RG27: H Win 1J 13
Poors Farm Rd.
RG24: Old B 1C 18
POPHAM **7B 34**
Popham La. RG25: N Wal . . .2C 34
Poplar Cl. RG27: Sher L 6G 5
POPLEY **1E 16**
Popley Way RG24: B'toke . .1E 16
Poppy Cl. SP10: A'ver 7B 36
Poppy Fld. RG24: Lych 1J 17
Porchester Ct. SP10: Charl . .3C 36
Porchester Sq.
RG21: B'toke 4D 16
(off Festival Pl.)
Portacre Ri. RG21: B'toke . . .6B 16
Portal Cl. SP11: A'ver 7A 36
Porter Cl. RG29: Odi 2C 28
Porter Rd. RG22: B'toke . . .1B 24
Porters Cl. RG25: Dumm . . .2H 35
SP10: A'ver 5C 36
Portland Gro. SP10: A'ver . . .6F 37

Portsmouth Cres.
RG22: B'toke 7K 15
Portsmouth Wlk.
RG22: B'toke 7K 15
Portsmouth Way
RG22: B'toke 7K 15
Portway Cl. SP10: A'ver 6C 36
Portway Ind. Est.
SP10: A'ver 5B 36
(East Portway, not continuous)
SP10: A'ver 5A 36
(Hopkinson Way)
Portway Pl. RG23: B'toke . . .4H 15
Portway Rdbt. SP10: A'ver . .4B 36
Post Horn La. RG27: Roth . .3J 11
Post Office La.
RG25: Dumm 2H 35
Potbridge Rd. RG29: Odi . . .2F 21
Pot La. RG24: Old B 2D 18
Potters La. RG27: Stra T 4J 5
Potters Wlk. RG21: B'toke . .4D 16
(off Festival Pl.)
Poultons Cl. RG25: Over 4C 32
Poultons Rd. RG25: Over . . .4C 32
Pound Cl. RG26: B'ley 4B 4
Pound Mdw. RG27: Sher L . .7H 5
RG28: Whit 6D 30
Pound Rd. RG25: Over 4D 32
Powerleague 1K 23
Powlingbroke RG27: Hoo . . .7D 12
Poynings Cres.
RG21: B'toke 7E 16
Poynters Cl. SP10: A'ver . . .4E 36
Poyntz Rd. RG25: Over 3C 32
Prescelly Cl. RG22: B'toke . .5H 15
Priest Down RG22: B'toke . .5H 23
Priestley Rd. RG24: B'toke . .1A 16
Primrose Ct. SP10: A'ver . . .1C 38
(off Floral Way)
Primrose Dr. RG27: H Win . .1K 13
Primrose Gdns.
RG22: B'toke 5H 23
Prince Albert Gdns.
SP10: A'ver 7F 37
(off Western Av.)
Prince Cl. SP10: A'ver 4J 37
Princes Cres.
RG22: B'toke 6A 16
Priors Row RG29: N War . . .5C 20
Priory Gdns. RG24: Old B . . .2K 17
Priory La. RG27: H Win 4H 13
RG28: Free 3G 31
Prisma Pk. RG24: B'toke . . .1G 17
Privett Cl. RG24: Lych 1J 17
Prospect Vs. RG27: B'toke . .7B 16
Puffin Cl. RG22: B'toke 4F 23
Purcell Cl. RG21: B'toke . . .1B 24
Puttenham Rd. RG24: Chin . . .5J 9
Pyotts Copse RG24: Old B . . .7J 9
Pyotts Ct. RG24: Old B 7J 9
PYOTT'S HILL **7J 9**
Pyott's Hill RG24: Old B 6J 9

Q

QM Sports Cen. **6D 16**
Quantock Cl.
RG22: B'toke 6H 15
Queen Anne's Wlk.
RG21: B'toke 4D 16
(off Festival Pl.)
Queen Mary Av.
RG21: B'toke 3D 16
Queens Av. SP10: A'ver 6F 37
Queensdale Ct.
RG21: B'toke 6C 16
(off Pittard Rd.)
Queensfield RG25: Dumm . .2H 35
Queens Mead Gdns.
RG29: Odi 6D 20
Queen's Pde.
RG21: B'toke 4D 16
Queens Rd. RG21: B'toke . . .4B 16
RG28: Whit 7D 30
RG29: N War 6C 20
Queensway SP10: A'ver 4J 37
QUIDHAMPTON **2E 32**
Quilter Rd. RG22: B'toke . . .1J 23

Quince Tree Way
RG27: Hoo 7B 12

R

Rack Cl. SP10: A'ver 6G 37
Radford Gdns.
RG21: B'toke 7B 16
Raglan Ct. RG22: B'toke . . .2J 23
Railway Cotts. RG23: Wort . .5F 15
RG24: Old B 3H 17
Rainbow Cl. RG24: Old B . . .4A 18
Rainham Cl. RG22: B'toke . . .3F 23
Ramparts, The
SP10: A'ver 1D 38
Rampton Rd. RG28: Whit . . .7D 30
RAMSDELL **1D 6**
Ramsdell Rd.
RG21: Cha A, M She . . .1F 7
Ramsholt Cl. RG25: N Wal . .1C 34
Rankine Rd. RG24: B'toke . .2F 17
Raphael Cl. RG21: B'toke . . .6F 17
Ravel Cl. RG22: B'toke 1A 24
Raven Cl. RG27: Hoo 7A 12
Ravenscroft RG27: Hoo 6B 12
Rawlings Rd. RG27: Hoo . . .1B 20
Rayleigh Rd. RG21: B'toke . .4C 16
Reading Rd.
RG24: B'toke, Chin 1F 17
(not continuous)
RG27: Matt, Roth 4B 12
RG27: Sher L 6H 5
Reading Rd. Roundabout
RG21: B'toke 2F 17
SP10: A'ver 6G 37
Rectory Rd. RG23: Oak 1A 22
RG24: B'toke 1A 20
Reculver Way SP10: Charl . .3C 36
Redbridge Dr. SP10: A'ver . .7E 36
Redbridge La.
RG24: Old B 4G 17
Redes Cl. RG27: Hoo 7D 12
RG25: Over 3C 32
Red Lion La. RG21: B'toke . .5D 16
Red Lion M. RG29: Odi 6E 20
Redon Way SP10: A'ver 5E 36
RED RICE **6A 38**
Red Rice Rd.
SP11: Red R, Up C 6A 38
Redwing Rd. RG22: B'toke . .3F 23
Redwood RG24: Chin 5G 9
Regal Hgts. RG29: Odi 6D 20
Regent Cl. RG21: B'toke 3E 16
Regents Ct. SP10: A'ver 5K 37
Reith Way SP10: A'ver 5A 36
Rembrandt Cl.
RG21: B'toke 6F 17
Remembrance Gdns.
RG24: Chin 6G 9
Rennie Ga. SP10: A'ver 5B 36
Renoir Cl. SP10: A'ver 6F 17
Renown Way RG24: Chin . . .4H 9
Restormel Cl.
RG23: B'toke 3H 15
Reynolds Cl. RG21: B'toke . .5G 17
Reynolds Cl. SP10: A'ver . . .4E 36
Reynolds Ho. RG22: B'toke . .7J 15
(off Pinkerton Rd.)
Reyntiens Vw. RG29: Odi . . .7E 20
Rhodes Sq. SP10: A'ver 3H 37
Ribble Way RG21: B'toke . . .4F 17
Richards Fld. RG24: Old B . . .6J 9
Richardson Cl. RG26: B'ley . .5C 4
Richborough Dr.
SP10: Charl 3B 36
Richmond Rd.
RG21: B'toke 3C 16
Rickett La. RG27: H Wes . . .1H 11
Ridge Cl. RG22: B'toke 5J 23
Ridge La. RG27: Newn 7H 11
Ridleys Piece
RG29: S War 6A 28
Riley La. RG24: Old B 2K 17
Ringshall Gdns.
RG26: B'ley 4B 4
Ringway Cen., The
RG21: B'toke 2B 16
Ringway E. RG21: B'toke . . .2F 17

Ringway Ho. RG24: B'toke . . .2F 17
Ringway Nth.
RG21: B'toke 2J 15
Ringway Sth. RG21: B'toke . .7C 16
Ringway W. RG21: B'toke . . .2A 16
Ripley Ter. RG27: Sher L 3K 9
Riverside SP11: G Cla 5F 39
Riverside Cl. RG24: Old B . . .1K 17
RG25: Over 3D 32
River Way SP10: A'ver 4G 37
Robert Mays Rd.
RG29: Odi 7C 20
Robin Cl. RG21: B'toke 2G 23
Robin Way SP10: A'ver 4G 37
Rochester Cl.
RG22: B'toke 2H 23
Rochford Rd. RG21: B'toke . .4C 16
Rockbourne Rd.
RG27: Sher L 3J 9
Roding Cl. RG22: B'toke . . .4F 17
Rodney Ct. SP10: A'ver 5J 37
Roentgen Rd.
RG21: B'toke 2G 17
Roke La. RG29: Odi 1G 29
Roman Ho. RG23: B'toke . . .4H 15
Roman Rd.
RG23: B'toke, Wort 5G 15
Roman Way RG23: Wort 5G 15
SP10: A'ver 2G 37
Romsey Cl. RG24: B'toke 7C 8
Romsey Rd.
SP11: G Cla, Wher 6H 39
Rookery, The RG28: Whit . . .6C 30
Rooksbury Rd. SP10: A'ver . .1D 38
Rooksdown Av.
RG24: B'toke 1J 15
Rooksdown La.
RG24: B'toke 1H 15
(not continuous)
Rookswood Cl. RG27: Hoo . . .7B 12
Rosebay Gdns. RG27: Hoo . .6C 12
Roseberry Cl.
RG22: B'toke 5H 23
Rose Cl. RG22: B'toke 2H 23
Rose Est., The RG27: Hoo . .1B 20
Rosefield Cl. RG27: H Win . .1K 13
Rosehip Way RG24: Lych . . .2H 17
Rose Hodson Pl.
RG23: B'toke 2J 15
Rosewood RG24: Chin 5G 9
Ross Cl. RG22: B'toke 7C 16
Rossini Cl. RG22: B'toke . . .2A 24
Rothay Ct. RG21: B'toke . . .4F 17
ROTHERWICK 3J 11
Rotherwick La.
RG27: H Wes, Roth 1F 11
Rotten Hill RG25: Over 5J 31
RG28: Lave 5J 31
Roundmead Rd.
RG21: B'toke 5C 16
Roundtown RG25: Tun 2K 25
Roundway Ct. SP10: A'ver . .6D 36
Row, The RG27: H Win 2K 13
(off High St.)
Rowner Cres. RG27: Sher L . .3J 9
Royal Cl. RG22: B'toke 5G 23
Royce Cl. SP10: A'ver 5A 36
Rubens Cl. RG21: B'toke . . .7F 17
Rune Dr. SP10: A'ver 2E 36
Rushes, The RG21: B'toke . .4F 17
Ruskin Cl. RG21: B'toke . . .6G 17
Russell Rd. RG21: B'toke . . .6D 16
Rutherford Rd.
RG24: B'toke 1F 17
Rycroft Mdw. RG22: B'toke . .6G 23
Rydal Cl. RG22: B'toke 7G 15
Ryon Cl. SP10: A'ver 2F 37

S

Saffron Cl. RG24: Chin 4J 9
Sainfoin La. RG23: Oak 2B 22
(not continuous)
Sainsbury Cl. SP10: A'ver . . .1E 38
St Alphege Gdns.
SP10: A'ver 4E 36
St Andrew's Rd.
RG22: B'toke 6K 15
(not continuous)

St Annes Cl.—Swift Cl.

St Annes Cl. SP11: G Cla 6E **38**
St Ann's Cl. SP10: A'ver 7E **36**
St Barbara's Cl. RG26: B'ley 5E **4**
St Birinus Gdns. SP10: A'ver 3E **36**
St Birstan Gdns. SP10: A'ver 4E **36**
St Christophers Cl. RG22: B'toke 6J **15**
St Davids Cl. RG29: Odi 7C **20**
St David's Rd. RG22: B'toke 6A **16**
St Gabriels Lea RG24: Chin 5J **9**
St Hubert Rd. SP10: A'ver 7D **36**
St James' Cl. RG26: B'ley 5E **4**
St John Cl. RG26: B'ley 5D **4**
St John's Cl. RG27: Hoo 7B **12**
St John's Cotts. RG27: Hoo 1J **19**
St John's Piece RG23: Oak 2B **22**
St Johns Rd. RG23: Oak 7B **14**
RG27: H Win 3K **13**
SP10: A'ver 6G **37**
St Johns Wlk. *RG21: B'toke 4D **16***
(off Festival Pl.)
St Joseph's Cres. RG24: Chin 6H **9**
St Leonards Av. RG24: Chin 5J **9**
St Lukes Cl. RG22: B'toke 6J **15**
St Marks Cl. RG26: B'ley 5D **4**
St Mary's Av. RG26: B'ley 5E **4**
St Mary's Cl. RG24: Old B 3K **17**
St Mary's Ct. RG21: B'toke 4E **16**
RG26: B'ley 5E **4**
St Mary's Mdw. SP11: Abb A 3A **38**
St Mary's Rd. RG27: H Win 3J **13**
St Michael's Cl. RG25: N Wal 2B **34**
ST MICHAEL'S HOSPICE 7A **8**
St Michael's Rd. RG22: B'toke 6J **15**
St Nicholas Ct. RG22: B'toke 5K **15**
St Patrick's Rd. RG22: B'toke 6A **16**
St Paul's Rd. RG22: B'toke 6A **16**
St Peter's Cl. SP11: G Cla 5G **39**
St Peter's Rd. RG22: B'toke 5J **15**
St Stephen's Cl. RG27: U Nat 4F **19**
St Swithin Way SP10: A'ver 4E **36**
St Thomas Cl. RG21: B'toke 2C **16**
SP10: Charl 3D **36**
Salisbury Cl. RG29: Odi 7C **20**
Salisbury Gdns. RG22: B'toke 5J **15**
Salisbury Rd. SP10: A'ver 1C **38**
SP11: Abb A, Ann V 5A **38**
Salmond Rd. SP11: A'ver 6A **36**
Salmons Rd. RG29: Odi 7C **20**
SALTERS HEATH 1K **7**
Salters Heath Rd. RG26: M She 2H **7**
Sam Whites Hill SP11: Up C 3D **38**
Sandbanks Dr. RG22: B'toke 3H **23**
Sandpiper Way RG22: B'toke 3F **23**
Sandringham Ct. RG22: B'toke 6K **15**
Sandringham Ho. SP10: A'ver 3F **37**
Sandy La. RG27: H Win 3K **13**
Sandys Cl. RG22: B'toke 6A **16**
Sandys Rd. RG22: B'toke 5A **16**
Sandys Rd. Roundabout RG22: B'toke 5A **16**
Saor M. SP10: A'ver 6E **36**
Sapley La. RG25: Over 4C **32**
Sarum Hill RG21: B'toke 5C **16**
Sarum Ho. SP10: A'ver 7F **37**
Savoy Cinema 7G **37**
Savoy Cl. SP10: A'ver 7G **37**
Saxon Ct. SP10: A'ver 3F **37**
Saxon Way RG24: Lych 2H **17**
SP10: A'ver 3E **36**
Scarlatti Rd. RG22: B'toke 2B **24**
Sceptre Ct. SP10: A'ver 5K **37**
Schroeder Cl. RG21: B'toke 7C **16**
Schubert Rd. RG22: B'toke 2A **24**
Scotney Rd. RG21: B'toke 2D **16**
Scots Ct. RG27: Hoo 6C **12**
Scott Cl. SP10: A'ver 5K **37**
Scott Ho. RG21: B'toke 3E **16**
Scures Rd. RG27: Hoo 7K **11**
Seagull Cl. RG22: B'toke 2F **23**
Seal Rd. RG21: B'toke 4D **16**
Searl's La. RG27: Hoo, Roth 4B **12**
(not continuous)
Seeviours Ct. RG28: Whit 6C **30**
Selborne Cl. RG27: Hoo 7B **12**
Selby Wlk. RG24: B'toke 7D **8**
Seton Dr. RG27: Hoo 1K **19**
Seventon Rd. RG25: N Wal 2C **34**
Severals, The RG24: Sher J 5A **8**
Severn Gdns. RG23: Oak 1B **22**
Severn Way RG21: B'toke 4F **17**
Seville Cres. SP10: A'ver 5H **37**
(not continuous)
Seymour Ct. *RG29: Odi 6E **20***
(off Seymour Pl.)
Seymour Pl. RG29: Odi 6E **20**
Seymour Rd. RG22: B'toke 7J **15**
Shackleton Sq. *SP10: A'ver 3H **37***
(off Cricketers Way)
Shakespeare Av. SP10: A'ver 5C **36**
Shakespeare Rd. RG24: B'toke 1E **16**
Shapley Heath RG27: Win 6H **13**
Shaw Cl. SP10: A'ver 6B **36**
Shaw Pightle RG27: Hoo 7K **11**
Sheep Fair SP10: A'ver 6H **37**
Sheep Fair Cl. SP10: A'ver 6H **37**
Sheepwash La. RG26: Rams 2D **6**
Sheldon's La. RG27: Hoo 7K **11**
Sheldons Rd. RG27: Hoo 7A **12**
Shelley Cl. RG24: B'toke 1E **16**
Shepherds Row SP10: A'ver 7H **37**
Shepherds Spring La. SP10: A'ver 6F **37**
Shepherds Spting Cotts. SP10: A'ver 4F **37**
Sheppard Cl. RG28: Whit 7C **30**
Sheppard Rd. RG21: B'toke 7C **16**
Sheppard Sq. *SP10: A'ver 4H **37***
(off Cricketers Way)
Sheraton Av. RG22: B'toke 3H **23**
Sherborne Rd. RG21: B'toke 2C **16**
RG24: Sher J 5A **8**
SHERBORNE ST JOHN 5A **8**
SHERFIELD GREEN 6G **5**
SHERFIELD ON LODDON 7G **5**
Sherfield Rd. RG26: B'ley 4C **4**
RG27: Sher L 5D **4**
Sherrington Way RG22: B'toke 7B **16**
Sherwood Cl. RG22: B'toke 4J **23**
Shetland Rd. RG24: B'toke 7E **8**
Shipton Way RG22: B'toke 7J **15**
Shooters Way RG21: B'toke 3E **16**
Shortwood Copse La. RG22: B'toke 5F **23**
Sibelius Cl. RG22: B'toke 3A **24**
Sidlaw Cl. RG22: B'toke 6G **15**
Sidmouth Rd. SP10: A'ver 6H **37**
Silchester Cl. SP10: A'ver 4D **36**
Silchester Rd. RG26: B'ley 5A **4**
Silk Mill La. RG25: Over 3B **32**
Silkweavers Rd. SP10: A'ver 6G **37**
Silver Birch Rd. SP10: A'ver 5D **36**
Silvester Cl. RG21: B'toke 2E **16**
Simmons Wlk. RG21: B'toke 5E **16**
Simons Cl. RG24: Chin 6H **9**
Simons Rd. RG24: Chin 6G **9**
Sims Cl. RG26: B'ley 5E **4**
Skippetts La. E. RG21: B'toke 7E **16**
Skippetts La. W. RG21: B'toke 7D **16**
Skylark Cl. RG22: B'toke 4F **23**
Skylark Ri. RG28: Whit 5B **30**
Slessor Cl. SP11: A'ver 7A **36**
Smallfield Dr. RG27: Hoo 7C **12**
Smannell Rd. SP10: A'ver 3G **37**
SP11: Sman 3G **37**
Smannell Rd. Rdbt. SP10: A'ver 4F **37**
Smeaton Rd. SP10: A'ver 5A **36**
Smith's Fld. RG25: Over 4D **32**
Smiths Mead RG25: N Wal 2D **34**
Smithy, The RG26: B'ley 4C **4**
Snowdrop Cl. RG22: B'toke 2G **23**
Sobers Sq. SP10: A'ver 3H **37**
Solby's Rd. RG21: B'toke 4C **16**
Solent Dr. RG22: B'toke 3H **23**
Somerville Ct. SP10: A'ver 5J **37**
Sonning Cl. RG22: B'toke 3F **23**
Soper Gro. RG21: B'toke 3D **16**
Sopers Row RG24: Old B 3J **17**
Sopwith Pk. SP10: A'ver 5A **36**
Sorrell's Cl. RG24: Chin 5H **9**
South Dr. RG27: Sher L 2B **10**
South End Rd. SP10: A'ver 1G **39**
Southend Rd. RG21: B'toke 4C **16**
Southern Haye RG27: H Win 3J **13**
Southern Rd. RG21: B'toke 5D **16**
SOUTH HAM 6A **16**
Sth. Ham Ho. RG22: B'toke 6J **15**
Sth. Ham Rd. RG22: B'toke 5A **16**
South Hill RG25: Up G 5G **27**
SOUTHINGTON 3B **32**
Southington Cl. RG25: Over 4B **32**
Southington La. RG25: Over 3B **32**
Southlands RG24: Chin 5G **9**
Southlea RG25: Clid 2C **24**
South Ridge RG29: Odi 7E **20**
South St. SP10: A'ver 1F **39**
SOUTH VIEW 2D **16**
South Vw. Cotts. RG27: Hoo 7A **12**
South Vw. Gdns. SP10: A'ver 7G **37**
Southview M. RG21: B'toke 2E **16**
SOUTH WARNBOROUGH 7A **28**
South Way SP10: A'ver 4J **37**
SPANISH GREEN 5K **5**
Speckled Wood Rd. RG24: B'toke 7D **8**
Sperrin Cl. RG22: B'toke 6H **15**
Spey Ct. SP10: A'ver 4H **37**
Spindlewood RG24: Chin 4G **9**
Spinney, The RG24: B'toke 2A **16**
RG27: Hoo 6A **12**
Sports Cen., The 4D **16**
Sprat's Hatch La. RG27: Dogm, Win 3K **21**
Sprents La. RG25: Over 4D **32**
Spring Cl. RG24: Sher J 4A **8**
Springfield RG23: Oak 7C **14**
Springfield Av. RG27: H Win 1J **13**
Springfield Cl. SP10: A'ver 6J **37**
Spring M. *SP10: A'ver 5G **37***
(off Shepherds Spring La.)
Springpark Ho. RG21: B'toke 3E **16**
Spruce Cl. SP10: A'ver 7B **36**
Square, The RG21: B'toke 3E **16**
Squarefield Gdns. RG27: Hoo 6C **12**
Squirrel Dr. RG23: B'toke 7F **23**
Stable Cl. RG27: Hoo 7K **11**
Stag Hill RG22: B'toke 7K **15**
Stag Oak La. RG24: Chin 4G **9**
Stanford Rd. RG22: B'toke 2J **23**
Starling Cl. RG22: B'toke 2F **23**
Statham Sq. SP10: A'ver 3H **37**
Station App. RG21: B'toke 3D **16**
SP10: A'ver 6D **36**
Station Downside RG27: Win 7K **13**
Station Hill RG21: B'toke 3D **16**
RG25: Over 1D **32**
RG27: Win 6J **13**
Station Mall RG21: B'toke 4D **16**
Station Rd. RG23: Oak 7A **14**
RG25: Clid 3C **24**
RG25: Over 3D **32**
RG27: Hoo 7A **12**
RG27: Win 7K **13**
RG28: Whit 5C **30**
Stephenson Cl. SP10: A'ver 5B **36**
Stephenson Rd. RG21: B'toke 3A **16**
Sterling Pk. SP10: A'ver 5B **36**
STEVENTON 7K **33**
Stewart Rd. RG24: B'toke 7G **9**
Stiles Dr. SP10: A'ver 6J **37**
Stockbridge Cl. RG24: Chin 4K **9**
Stockbridge Rd. RG25: N Wal 4B **34**
SP11: Red R 7A **38**
Stocker Cl. RG21: B'toke 7C **16**
Stoken La. RG27: H Win 1F **13**
Stokes La. RG24: Sher J 5H **7**
RG26: M She 5H **7**
Stone Cl. SP10: A'ver 1D **38**
Stonehills RG25: Stev 6J **33**
Stonelea Gro. RG29: N War 3C **20**
Stourhead Cl. SP10: A'ver 7D **36**
Stour Rd. RG23: Oak 1B **22**
Stratfield Rd. RG21: B'toke 2C **16**
Stratfield Saye Rd. RG7: Stra S 2D **4**
STRATFIELD TURGIS 3K **5**
Strathfield Rd. SP10: A'ver 2E **38**
Stratton Rd. RG21: B'toke 7B **16**
Strauss Rd. RG22: B'toke 2J **23**
Stravinsky Rd. RG22: B'toke 2B **24**
Strawberry Flds. RG26: B'ley 3C **4**
Street, The RG24: Old B 3J **17**
RG26: B'ley 5A **4**
RG27: Roth 3J **11**
RG29: Grey 7K **19**
RG29: L Sut 7D **28**
RG29: N War 6B **20**
STREET END 2K **11**
Stroud Cl. RG24: Chin 6G **9**
Stroud Grn. La. RG27: Roth 4G **11**
Stroudley Rd. RG24: B'toke 1G **17**
Stuart Ct. SP10: A'ver 3F **37**
Stubbs Ct. SP10: A'ver 4E **36**
Stubbs Rd. RG21: B'toke 7E **16**
Stukeley Rd. RG21: B'toke 5B **16**
Suffolk Rd. SP10: A'ver 7E **36**
Sullivan Rd. RG22: B'toke 2A **24**
Summerfields RG24: Chin 4J **9**
Sunflower Cl. RG22: B'toke 3H **23**
Sunny Mead RG23: Oak 2B **22**
Sunnyside Cl. SP10: Charl 4C **36**
Sutcliffe Sq. *SP10: A'ver 3H **37***
(off Cricketers Way)
Sutherland Ct. *SP10: A'ver 5F **37***
(off Artists Way)
Sutton Rd. RG21: B'toke 2D **16**
Swallow Cl. RG22: B'toke 2F **23**
Swallowfields SP10: A'ver 3G **37**
Swan Ct. RG27: H Win 2K **13**
Swan M. RG29: N War 5C **20**
Swift Cl. SP10: A'ver 4G **37**

Welton Ct. RG21: B'toke 4C 16
Wentworth Cres.
   RG22: B'toke 5G 23
Wesley Wlk. *RG21: B'toke . . .4D 16*
   (off Festival Pl.)
Wessex Av. RG29: Odi 1D 28
Wessex Cl. RG21: B'toke 6C 16
Wessex Cres. RG29: Odi 1D 28
Wessex Dr. RG29: Odi 1D 28
Wessex Gdns. SP10: A'ver . . .6E 36
Wessex Grange
   RG27: Sher L 7H 5
Westbrook Cl. RG23: Oak . . .2B 22
Westbrook Ct. RG22: Wort . . .5G 15
Westbrooke Cl.
   SP10: A'ver 7F 37
Westdeane Ct.
   RG21: B'toke 5B 16
West End RG24: Sher J 4K 7
Western Av. SP10: A'ver 6F 37
Western Cross RG29: Odi 7D 20
Western La. RG29: Odi 6D 20
Western Rd. SP10: A'ver 7F 37
Western Way
   RG22: B'toke 7K 15
   RG22: B'toke 7G 37
Westfield Rd.
   RG21: B'toke 6E 16
Westgate Cl. RG23: B'toke . . .3H 15
WEST GREEN 3F 13
West Green House Gdns. . . .3F 13
West Grn. Rd.
   RG27: H Win 1F 13
WEST HAM 4K 15
W. Ham Cl. RG22: B'toke 5J 15
West Ham Ct.
   RG22: B'toke 5J 15
West Ham Est.
   RG22: B'toke 5A 16
W. Ham La. RG22: B'toke 4K 15
   RG22: Wort 5H 15
West Ham Rdbt.
   RG22: B'toke 5K 15
Westlands Ho.
   RG21: B'toke 5C 16
West La. RG29: N War 4B 20
Westmarch Bus. Cen.
   SP10: A'ver 4G 37
Westminster Cl.
   RG22: B'toke 3H 23
Westminster Ho.
   RG21: B'toke 4D 16
   (off Festival Pl.)
Weston Cl. RG25: Up G 5F 27
WESTON CORBETT 7D 26
WESTON PATRICK 7E 26
Weston Rd. RG25: Up G 6E 26
W. Point Bus. Pk.
   SP10: A'ver 5A 36
West Portway SP10: A'ver . . .4A 36
Westray Cl. RG21: B'toke 2F 17
Westside Cl. RG22: B'toke . . .6K 15
West St. RG29: N War, Odi . . .6B 20
   SP10: A'ver 6F 37
   (not continuous)
West Vw. SP10: A'ver 5A 36
West Way SP10: A'ver 5J 37
Wetherby Gdns.
   SP10: Charl 4D 36
Weybrook Ct. RG24: Sher J . .4K 7
Weyhill Rd. SP10: A'ver 6B 36
   SP11: A'ver, Pen C 5A 36

Weysprings Cl.
   RG21: B'toke 4F 17
Wharf, The RG29: Odi 5F 21
Wheatleys Cl. RG25: Stev . . .7J 33
Wheeler Cl. RG28: Whit 7D 30
Wheelers Hill RG27: Hoo . . .7C 12
Whinchat Cl. RG27: H Win . . .1J 13
Whistler Cl. RG21: B'toke . . .6F 17
WHITCHURCH 6C 30
Whitchurch Silk Mill 7C 30
Whitchurch Station (Rail) . .5C 30
White Hart La.
   RG21: B'toke 5E 16
   RG26: Cha A 1E 6
Whitehead Cl. RG24: Lych . .2H 17
White Hill RG29: Wel 7G 29
White Ho. Cl.
   RG22: B'toke 7K 15
White La. RG25: Up G 1F 27
   RG25: W Cor 7C 26
White Oak Way
   SP11: Ann V 3B 38
Whites Cl. RG27: Hoo 7K 11
Whitestones RG22: B'toke . .4J 23
Whitewater Ri. RG27: Hoo . .6C 12
Whitewater Rd.
   RG29: N War 5C 20
Whitewood RG24: Chin 5H 9
Whitgift Cl. RG22: B'toke . . .5H 23
Whitmarsh La. RG24: Chin . .5K 9
   RG27: Sher L 5K 9
Whitney Rd. RG24: B'toke . .2G 17
Whittle Rd. SP10: A'ver 5A 36
Whynot La. SP10: A'ver 6D 36
Wickham Way
   RG27: Sher L 3K 9
Wicklow Cl. RG22: B'toke . . .6H 15
Widmore Rd. RG22: B'toke . .7J 15
Wights Wlk. RG22: B'toke . . .3H 23
Wild Herons RG27: Hoo 7C 12
WILDMOOR 3D 10
Wildmoor La.
   RG27: Sher L 7H 5
Willis Mus., The 5D 16
Willoughby Way
   RG23: B'toke 3K 15
Willow Gro. SP10: A'ver 7E 36
Willows, The
   RG29: N War 5C 20
   SP10: A'ver 1E 38
Willow Way RG23: B'toke . . .2K 15
   RG27: Sher L 6G 5
Wilmott Way
   RG23: B'toke 3K 15
Wilton Pl. RG21: B'toke 5B 16
Wimborne Cl.
   RG22: B'toke 5G 23
Winchcombe Rd.
   RG21: B'toke 5C 16
Winchester Gdns.
   SP10: A'ver 1G 39
Winchester Rd.
   RG21: B'toke 6B 16
   RG22: B'toke 6E 22
   RG23: B'toke 6E 22
   RG28: Whit 7C 30
   SP10: A'ver 2F 39
   (not continuous)
   SP11: A'ver, Wher, G Cla
   . . . . .6H 39
Winchester Rd. Roundabout
   RG21: B'toke 6B 16

Winchester St.
   RG21: B'toke 5D 16
   RG25: Over 3D 32
   RG28: Whit 6C 30
   SP10: A'ver 7F 37
WINCHFIELD 6J 13
Winchfield Station (Rail) . .6J 13
Windermere Av.
   RG22: B'toke 7G 15
Windmill La. SP11: Ann V . . .3B 38
Windover St.
   RG21: B'toke 5D 16
   (off New St.)
Windrush Cl. *RG21: B'toke . . .4F 17*
   (off Severn Way)
Windsor Gdns.
   RG22: B'toke 4G 23
Windsor Rd. SP10: A'ver 6E 36
Wingate La. RG29: L Sut 7D 28
WINKLEBURY 2J 15
Winklebury Cen.
   RG23: B'toke 4J 15
Winklebury Way
   RG23: B'toke 4H 15
WINSLADE 5H 25
Winslade La. RG25: Elli 7F 25
Winterbourne Ho.
   RG22: B'toke 7J 15
   (off Pinkerton Rd.)
Winterdyne M.
   SP10: A'ver 7E 36
Winterthur Way
   RG21: B'toke 4C 16
Winton Chase SP10: A'ver . .6J 37
Winton Sq. RG21: B'toke . . .5D 16
Wisley Rd. SP10: A'ver 7C 36
Wistaria Ct. SP10: A'ver 7C 36
Witan Cl. SP10: A'ver 2G 37
Witan Ct. RG28: Whit 5B 30
Wither Ri. RG23: Oak 7A 14
Woburn Gdns.
   RG22: B'toke 6J 15
Wolds, The RG22: B'toke . . .6H 15
Wolversdene Cl.
   SP10: A'ver 7H 37
Wolversdene Gdns.
   SP10: A'ver 7H 37
Wolversdene Rd.
   SP10: A'ver 7G 37
Woodbury Rd.
   RG22: B'toke 3H 23
Wood Cl. RG22: B'toke 4H 23
Woodcroft RG23: Oak 2B 22
Wood End RG24: Chin 6G 9
Woodgarston Dr.
   RG22: B'toke 4G 23
Woodgarston La.
   RG26: Up W 1C 14
Wood Hill La.
   RG29: L Sut, Odi 6D 28
Woodland Ct.
   RG22: B'toke 5F 23
Woodland Dr. RG26: B'ley . . .5E 4
Woodlands RG24: Chin 4J 9
   RG25: Over 3C 32
Woodlands Bus. Village
   RG21: B'toke 3F 17
Woodlands Way
   SP10: A'ver 6H 37
Wood La. RG27: U Nat 4G 19
Woodmanfield
   RG25: Up G 5G 27

Woodmere Cft.
   RG22: B'toke 3F 23
Woodpecker Cl.
   RG22: B'toke 2F 23
Woodroffe Dr.
   RG22: B'toke 1J 23
Woodside Gdns.
   RG24: Chin 4J 9
Woods La. RG25: Clid 3A 24
   RG29: Grey 5K 19
Woodstock Mead
   RG22: B'toke 4H 23
Woodville Cl. RG24: Chin . . .5H 9
Woodville La. RG24: Chin . . .6H 9
Woodville Ri. RG24: Chin . . .6H 9
Wood Wlk. RG26: Rams 3A 6
Wooldridge Cres.
   RG29: Odi 2C 28
Woolford Way
   RG23: B'toke 3K 15
Wool Gro. SP10: A'ver 7H 37
Woolley Sq. SP10: A'ver 3H 37
Wootton Cl. RG23: W Law . . .2F 15
Wootton La.
   RG23: W Law 5D 14
   RG26: Up W 7C 6
WOOTTON ST LAWRENCE . . .2E 14
Worcester Av.
   RG22: B'toke 3H 23
Wordsworth Cl.
   RG22: B'toke 1E 16
Worrell Sq. *SP10: A'ver 3H 37*
   (off Cricketers Way)
Worsam Ct. RG22: B'toke . . .5H 15
WORTING 5G 15
Worting Rd. RG21: B'toke . . .5K 15
   RG22: B'toke 5J 15
   RG23: Newf, Wort 6C 14
Worting Rd. Roundabout
   RG22: B'toke 5J 15
Wote St. RG21: B'toke 5D 16
Wrekin Cl. RG22: B'toke 6H 15
Wrens Cl. RG22: B'toke 2F 23
Wye Cl. SP10: A'ver 4J 37
Wykeham Ct. RG29: Odi 2D 28
Wykeham Dr.
   RG23: Wort 5G 15
   (not continuous)
Wyndham Rd. SP10: A'ver . . .1D 38

Y

Yellowhammer Rd.
   RG22: B'toke 3F 23
Yew Tree Cl. RG23: Oak 2B 22
   RG26: B'ley 5D 4
   SP11: G Cla 6F 39
Yew Tree Rd.
   RG25: N Wal 2C 34
York Cl. RG22: B'toke 2H 23
York Ct. SP10: A'ver 3F 37
York Ho. RG22: B'toke 6A 16
York La. RG27: H Win 3J 13

Z

Zinnia Cl. RG22: B'toke 4G 23